China in the Middle East

The Wary Dragon

Andrew Scobell, Alireza Nader

Prepared for the United States Army
Approved for public release; distribution unlimited

For more information on this publication, visit www.rand.org/t/RR1229

Library of Congress Cataloging-in-Publication Data is available for this publication.
ISBN: 978-0-8330-9194-9

Published by the RAND Corporation, Santa Monica, Calif.

Cover: Photo by Fred Dufour/Associated Press.

Preface

This research is part of the fiscal year 2014 project "China Pivots to the Middle East." The project examined China's economic, political, and military roles in the Middle East and provided insights to help inform U.S. Army decisions regarding presence and force posture in the region.

This report examines China's interests in and strategy toward the Middle East. Specifically, the report explores China's economic, political, and security role in the region, with particular attention to China's relations with Saudi Arabia and Iran. Finally, the report contemplates the consequences of the Chinese strategy toward the Middle East for the United States and, more specifically, the U.S. Army. The research and writing of the report were completed in October 2014.

This research was sponsored by Deputy Chief of Staff, G-8, U.S. Army, and conducted within the RAND Arroyo Center's Strategy, Doctrine, and Resources Program. RAND Arroyo Center, part of the RAND Corporation, is a federally funded research and development center sponsored by the United States Army.

The Project Unique Identification Code (PUIC) for the project that produced this document is HQD136620.

Contents

Preface ... iii
Figures ... vii
Summary ... ix
Acknowledgments ... xi

CHAPTER ONE
Introduction ... 1

CHAPTER TWO
How Important to China Is the Middle East? ... 3
History ... 3
Does China Have a Middle East Strategy? ... 5
China's Interests and Objectives in the Middle East ... 7
Conclusion ... 20

CHAPTER THREE
China Engages Saudi Arabia ... 23
Chinese Instruments and Mechanisms ... 24
Conclusion ... 45

CHAPTER FOUR
China and Iran—Close but Complicated ... 49
The Growth of Ties in the Wake of Iran's Revolution ... 53
Military and Nuclear Cooperation ... 55
Economic and Energy Cooperation ... 59
China and Sanctions ... 61

Relations Under Rouhani 64
Conclusion 71

CHAPTER FIVE
Whither the Wary Dragon? Implications for the United States 73
Mismatch in the Middle East...74
The Elephant in the Room 77
Recommendations 79

Abbreviations..85
References 87

Figures

2.1. Top Exporters of Petroleum to China, by Value 8
3.1. High-Level Chinese and U.S. Visits to Saudi Arabia 28
3.2. Saudi Petroleum Exports to the United States and China 36
3.3. SIPRI TIVs of Official Arms Exports to Saudi Arabia 42

Summary

This study examines China's economic, political, and security roles in the Middle East, focusing on China's relations with Saudi Arabia and Iran. The study explores what China is doing in the Middle East and why. Once considered by Beijing as a peripheral and relatively insignificant region of the world, the Middle East now looms much larger in China's national security calculus than ever before. Beijing's unprecedented interest and involvement in the Middle East raises the question of what is driving this activism. What explains China's increased attention to the Middle East, and what are the implications of this development for the United States?

The findings of this study suggest that Beijing is driven primarily by economic interests, as well as an attempt to "rebalance" its domestic, foreign, and security policies so that these are less skewed in favor of eastern China and East Asia. Greater interest and involvement in the Middle East are manifestations of growing dependence on energy resources from the region and Chinese efforts to "march west" into Central Asia and beyond. With the launch of the New Silk Road initiative, officially announced by President Xi Jinping in September 2013, Beijing's Middle East strategy was subsumed under a grand and highly ambitious effort to build the overland Silk Road Belt and the Maritime Silk Road linking China to the Middle East and beyond. While countering the United States is a factor, it is not the central driver of China's Middle East strategy.

This report recommends that the United States welcome some expanded Chinese security engagement in the Middle East. Indeed, given the region's vital importance to China's economy and China's growing power, Beijing might be receptive. And yet Beijing is very reluctant to expand its level of security cooperation with the United States or Middle East states because it fears being embroiled in regional tensions and controversies. China fears that greater security involvement would wreck its remarkable status as the one outside power on good terms with every major state in the Middle East. China is worried that greater diplomatic activism and security engagement in the region would come at the cost of blood, treasure, and an end to its reputation as friend to all and enemy of none. This study's focus on Beijing's relations with Riyadh and Tehran illuminates the scope and impact of greater Chinese involvement in the region but at the same time underscores the real limitations of China's Middle East strategy. Beijing has adopted a "wary dragon" strategy toward the region.

Expanded security cooperation between China and Saudi Arabia—building on robust economic ties, modest but cordial diplomatic relations, and limited military interactions—would not necessarily be cause for U.S. alarm. Such cooperation may be helpful and contribute toward a more stable regional environment. Greater Chinese security cooperation with Iran is more problematic, but there are no signs that Beijing is committed to building an alliance with Tehran, despite recent Chinese-Iranian naval exercises in the Persian Gulf. China is unlikely to attempt to "dominate" the region, even in the event of rising tensions between the United States and China over the Middle East. Rather, instability in the Middle East can provide a venue for greater U.S.-Chinese engagement, which might ultimately help alleviate rising tensions in East Asia. At a grand strategic level, Washington should adopt a two-part strategy where Beijing and the Middle East are concerned. First, the United States should encourage China, along with other Asian powers, to become more involved in efforts to improve regional stability. Second, Washington should work to reassure partners of its enduring security commitment to the region.

Acknowledgments

The authors would like to thank Tim Muchmore and Terrence Kelly for their insightful suggestions and constant encouragement. The authors also wish to express their appreciation to Sam Berkowitz, Astrid Cevallos, Cristina Garafola, James Hoobler, Ali Scotten, and Robert Stewart for invaluable research contributions.

The authors are also grateful to Jon Alterman, Dalia Dassa Kaye, and Scott Harold for their helpful peer reviews of the study.

CHAPTER ONE

Introduction

Once considered by the People's Republic of China (PRC) as a peripheral and relatively insignificant region of the world, the Middle East now looms much larger in China's national security calculus than ever before. Beijing's unprecedented interest and involvement in the Middle East raises the possibility that China has ambitious designs on the region. What explains China's increased attention to the Middle East, and what are the contours of engagement with the region?

One answer is that China is reacting to the U.S. "rebalance" to Asia, announced by the Obama administration in 2012. Another answer is that the Middle East is simply becoming increasingly important economically. Yet a third answer is that the region has become geostrategically far more important to Beijing. These last two answers suggest that the PRC's activities have little if anything to do with U.S. policy initiatives. This study contends that Beijing is primarily focused on energy security, as well as attempting to "rebalance" its domestic, foreign, and security policies so that these are less skewed in favor of eastern China and East Asia. This Beijing rebalance, however, is neither a reaction to the Obama administration's own rebalance nor a new phenomenon; nevertheless, the United States figures significantly in both major drivers, although China views the U.S. role very differently in each. In the context of China's quest for energy, the United States is perceived positively because it is a key guarantor of Middle East security through its military presence and considerable geopolitical influence, thereby helping to maintain stability and hence regional economic development and uninterrupted access to energy. In the context of China's broader security interests, the United States is perceived negatively because its alliances and forward military posture are viewed as threatening to China's security all around its periphery, especially in East Asia.

Does China have a strategy toward the Middle East? The findings of this report suggest that the answer is yes. China appears to have adopted a "wary dragon" strategy toward the region. Beijing exhibits a deep sense of vulnerability in its engagement with the Middle East. And China endeavors to protect its expanding interests in the region by assiduously avoiding taking sides in Middle East conflicts and controversies. Moreover, China is very cautious, alarmed about becoming embroiled in Middle East controversies or getting too close to any one country in the region. This strong aversion precludes the public articulation of a Middle East policy or strategy and the making of hard commitments to any states in the region beyond those that are required to maintain cordial business relations and pragmatic diplomatic and security ties. Chapter Two identifies China's evolving interests and objectives in the Middle East and explains why and how the region has become a high priority for Beijing in the post–Cold War era. This Middle East strategy is illuminated by focusing on China's use of the instruments of national power applied in its relationships with Saudi Arabia and Iran, two major powers that Beijing considers as pivotal in the region. Chapter Three examines China's burgeoning relationship with Saudi Arabia, a key U.S. partner in the region. Chapter Four explores China's enduring relationship with Iran, a major U.S. rival in the Middle East. Finally, Chapter Five assesses China's strategy toward the region and explores the implications for the United States and the U.S. Army. Because of Beijing's wary-dragon strategy, while China is growing in importance in the Middle East as an economic heavyweight, it persists as a diplomatic lightweight and is likely to remain a military featherweight in the region for the foreseeable future.

CHAPTER TWO

How Important to China Is the Middle East?

Today, the PRC attaches considerable importance to the Middle East. Although Beijing is primarily focused on internal security—as well as the stability of its immediate periphery, especially the Asia-Pacific region and Central Asia—it is nevertheless increasingly thinking and behaving in global terms.[1] Some regions of the world are more important than others. While there is no clear hierarchy, the Middle East looms larger for China in recent years than ever before. Why is the region important to China? Does Beijing have a strategy toward the Middle East? What are the key trends evident in China's involvement in the region? These questions are addressed in this chapter.

First, this chapter briefly reviews the history of PRC relations with the Middle East. Next, the chapter explores whether Beijing has a strategy toward the Middle East, and, if so, what this strategy might be. To this end, the chapter identifies key Chinese interests in the Middle East and describes Beijing's associated objectives.

History

A lesser power squeezed out by the two superpowers during the Cold War (1945–1991), the PRC was generally disengaged from the Middle East for much of that period. China had only a small presence and little

[1] Andrew J. Nathan and Andrew Scobell, *China's Search for Security*, New York: Columbia University Press, 2012.

at stake in the region.[2] By the 1980s, however, the PRC was more interested in gaining influence and expanding its presence in the Middle East—partly to compete with the United States and Soviet Union and partly in support of its efforts to gain greater international recognition at the expense of the rival Republic of China (ROC) in Taiwan.

PRC diplomatic wins in the Middle East came in the form of an initial trickle, followed by two waves of diplomatic normalizations. In 1956, Egypt and Syria became the first countries in the region to establish diplomatic relations with China. However, the real breakthrough occurred in the 1970s, following the PRC's admission into the United Nations and Beijing's assumption of the United Nations Security Council seat held by Taipei. Iran, Kuwait, and Lebanon all switched recognition from the ROC to the PRC in 1971, followed eventually by Jordan (1977) and Libya and Oman (1978). A second wave of Middle East diplomatic successes occurred between the mid-1980s and early 1990s. The United Arab Emirates normalized relations with the PRC in 1984, followed by Qatar in 1988, Bahrain in 1989, Saudi Arabia in 1990, and Israel in 1992.

China's interest in and economic dependence on the Middle East has skyrocketed since the 1990s and is likely to grow in future years. According to one international security analyst at China's most prominent think tank, the Central Party School in Beijing: "China's geopolitical, economic, energy, and security interests in the Middle East are continually expanding."[3] In contrast, U.S. commitment to and influence in the Middle East is perceived by some observers as decreasing. The withdrawal of U.S. troops from Iraq in 2011 and the draw-

---

[2] Evan S. Medeiros, *China's International Behavior: Activism, Opportunism, and Diversification*, Santa Monica, Calif.: RAND Corporation, MG-850-AF, 2009, pp. 160–161. For some authoritative overviews of China's involvement in the Middle East during the Cold War, see John Calabrese, "From Flyswatters to Silkworms: The Evolution of China's Role in West Asia," *Asian Survey*, Vol. 30, No. 9, September 1990; and Yitzhak Shichor, *The Middle East in China's Foreign Policy, 1949–1977*, New York: Cambridge University Press, 1979.

[3] Gao Zugui, "Dabianju shenhua beijingxia Zhongguo yu Zhong Dong guanxi de fazhan" ["Development of China's Relations with the Middle East in the Context of Profound Changes"], *Heping yu fazhan* [*Peace and Development*], No. 4, 2014, p. 45.

down of U.S. military forces from Afghanistan have contributed to this perception.[4]

A glance at some of the key powers in the Middle East illustrates the process. While the United States remains Saudi Arabia's most important security partner, Saudi Arabia is also becoming China's biggest source of imported oil and an increasingly important economic partner. Moreover, while Washington continues to be recognized as the most important capital city outside the region, Middle Eastern countries increasingly look to Beijing for trade, investments, diplomatic consultations, and even security cooperation. In addition, China has managed the impressive feat of maintaining good relations with virtually all countries in the region—including Iran, Saudi Arabia, and Israel—despite the long-standing and deep-seated animosity between those nations.[5]

Does China Have a Middle East Strategy?

The most obvious answer is that China does not have a strategy toward the Middle East because Beijing has not publicly articulated one.[6] Why? The reason is because of a desire to avoid controversy in, and blowback from, the region. As noted above, China maintains the remarkable status of an outside power that remains on good terms with all Middle

---

4 The real prospect of "a U.S. retreat from the region" is raised by Geoffrey Kemp. See his *The East Moves West: India, China, and Asia's Growing Presence in the Middle East*, Washington, D.C.: Brookings Institution, 2010, p. 18. These observers include Chinese analysts. See David Schenker, "China's Middle East Footprint," *Los Angeles Times*, April 27, 2013, p. 19; and Li Weijian, "Dangqian Zhong Dong anquan jushi ji dui Zhongguo Zhong Dong waijiao yingxiang" ["Current Security Situation in the Middle East and Implications for China's Middle East Diplomacy"], *Guoji guancha* [*International Observer*], No. 3, 2014.

5 Li Weijian, "Zhong Dong zai Zhongguo zhanlue zhong de zhongyaoxing ji shuangbian guanxi" [Bilateral Relations Between China and the Middle East and the Importance of the Middle East in China's Strategy"], *XiYa Feizhou* [*West Asia and Africa*], No. 6, 2004, p. 20. This is also noted by Kemp (2010, p. 67).

6 Indeed, most Chinese analysts insist that China does not have a Middle East strategy. Author interviews with Chinese civilian and military researchers in Beijing and Shanghai, September 2014 (hereafter "author interviews").

Eastern countries, and Beijing would prefer not to jeopardize this situation by articulating concrete policy positions or an explicit regional strategy. To do so would risk antagonizing or alienating one or more states—something China is loath to do.[7]

Beijing has been careful not to be seen as meddling in the internal political affairs of Middle Eastern states or taking very clear-cut positions on contentious regional issues. China's involvement in the Israel-Palestinian peace process, for example, has been negligible. And Beijing has shied away from joining the coalition against the Islamic State in Iraq and the Levant (ISIL).[8] One of China's overarching principles of foreign policy is "noninterference."

But if China does have an unarticulated strategy toward the Middle East—Beijing certainly takes the region very seriously—how would one know? China can be said to have a Middle East strategy if clear goals could be identified, based on explicit national interests, and if instruments of national power were used to advance these goals. Thus, one should be able to answer the following questions:

- What interests have been articulated by Beijing as being at stake in the Middle East?
- What objectives has China identified for the region?
- What instruments is China using in the Middle East and how are these employed?

The remainder of this chapter identifies China's key interests and related objectives in the Middle East. Then, by looking at how China has employed the instruments of national power at its disposal, Chap-

---

[7] Author interviews; author conversations with Chinese Middle East analysts in Washington, D.C., April 2015 (hereafter "author conversations").

[8] The organization's name transliterates from Arabic as al-Dawlah al-Islamiyah fi al-'Iraq wa al-Sham (abbreviated as Da'ish or DAESH). In the West, it is commonly referred to as the Islamic State of Iraq and the Levant (ISIL), the Islamic State of Iraq and Syria, the Islamic State of Iraq and the Sham (both abbreviated as ISIS), or simply as the Islamic State (IS). Arguments abound as to which is the most accurate translation, but here we refer to the group as ISIL.

ters Three and Four analyze how effective Beijing has been in implementing these interests and promoting these objectives.

China's Interests and Objectives in the Middle East

China's major interests in the Middle East are energy security, geostrategic ambitions, external linkages to internal stability, and enhanced great-power status. Beijing's corresponding objectives are ensuring access to energy and other resources, balancing against—but not directly opposing—U.S. influence, suppressing vocal and material support for China's minority Uighurs, and receiving explicit and implicit recognition from Middle Eastern states that China is a great power, respectively.

Energy Security

Beijing's foremost interest in the Middle East is continued access to energy resources.[9] China's remarkable sustained economic growth since the late 1970s has prompted a growing appetite for energy (and other natural resources). Oil is of increasing importance to China, which became a net energy importer in 1993. And, since 1995, the Middle East has been China's number one source of imported petroleum.[10]

According to one Chinese analyst writing in a prominent international affairs journal in 2014: "The Middle East will remain China's largest source of oil imports, and that is the strategic significance of the Middle East for China."[11] Petroleum is certainly central in China's bilateral ties with both Saudi Arabia and Iran. In 2012, Saudi Arabia was the number one source of petroleum (before Angola and Russia),

---

[9] See, for example, Chu Shulong and Jin Wei, *Zhongguo waijiao zhanlue he zhengce* [*China's Foreign Affairs Strategy and Policy*], Beijing: Shishi Chubanshe, 2008), pp. 263–264; author interviews.

[10] Jon B. Alterman and John W. Garver, *The Vital Triangle: China, the United States, and the Middle East*, Washington, D.C.: Center for Strategic and International Studies, 2008, p. 7, Figure 1.1.

[11] Niu Xinchun, "China's Interests in and Influence over the Middle East," trans. Haibing Xing, *Contemporary International Relations*, Vol. 24, No. 1, January/February 2014a, p. 39.

and Iran was the fourth most important source of imported Chinese oil. (See Figure 2.1.)

China also targets natural gas and commodities. In addition, Beijing actively pursues opportunities for investment and seeks contracts for infrastructure projects and access to new markets for Chinese products in the Middle East. Indeed, the New Silk Road initiative (often referred to as One Belt, One Road), officially launched by President Xi Jinping in 2013, is all-encompassing and seems to include all manner of economic activity and involvement in the region by the PRC government, state-owned corporations, and private companies and individual Chinese entrepreneurs.[12]

Geostrategy

China's second major interest in the Middle East is a desire to expand its geostrategic influence beyond the immediate Asia-Pacific neighborhood and develop relationships with other major or regional powers.

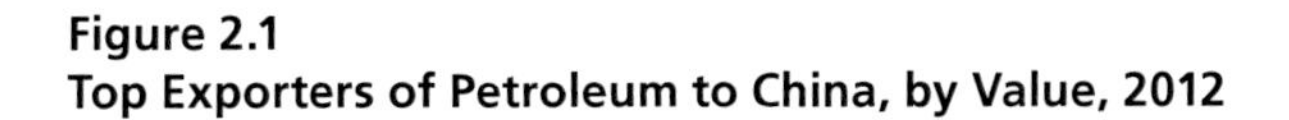

Figure 2.1
Top Exporters of Petroleum to China, by Value, 2012

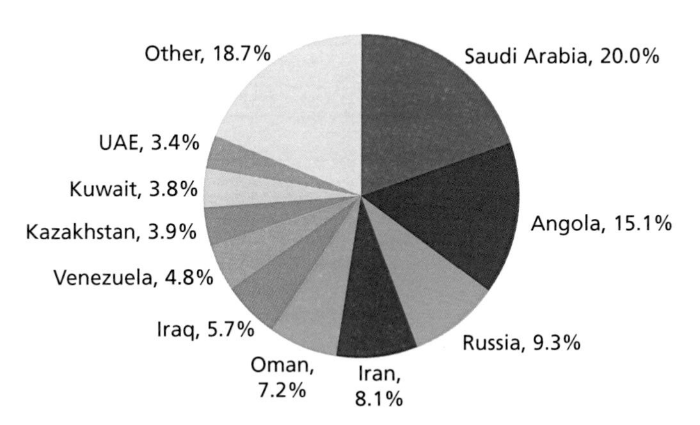

SOURCE: UN Comtrade Database, http://comtrade.un.org.
NOTE: UAE = United Arab Emirates.
RAND *RR1229-2.1*

---

[12] See "Vision and Actions Are Jointly Building Silk Road Economic Belt and 21st Century Maritime Silk Road," news release, National Development and Reform Commission, Ministry of Foreign Affairs, Ministry of Commerce of the People's Republic of China with State Council authorization, March 28, 2015.

Despite the assumption that China has become a world power, Beijing essentially remains a regional power with a global presence.[13] But this does not mean that China is bereft of global interests and aspirations. While Beijing is increasingly active around the world, certain regions are clearly more important to it than others. In the early 21st century, the Middle East may be the most important area of the globe outside the Asia-Pacific region for Beijing because of the Middle East's sizable energy resources and central geostrategic location.[14]

Marching West

As tensions between China and its neighbors have emerged in East Asia—including maritime territorial disputes in the East China and South China Seas—Chinese analysts and scholars have begun to assess the geostrategic situation and reevaluate Beijing's grand strategy, from a primary focus eastward toward the Pacific Ocean to a more balanced approach looking both east and west. Since 1978, when Chinese Communist Party (CCP) leaders adopted a policy of "reform and opening" to modernize China's moribund economy, Beijing's main strategic direction has been toward the maritime realm—to the East Asian littoral and beyond. It was here that the so-called four tiger economies of Hong Kong, Korea, Singapore, and Taiwan beckoned, and beyond them the larger economies of Japan and the United States. In the first three decades of economic reforms, the most-prosperous and most-modernized parts of the country were to be found along China's eastern seaboard, in such provinces as Guangdong and Fujian. This development was regionally uneven and left the country's interior behind. In an effort to remedy this imbalance, Beijing has poured substantial funds and considerable effort into developing the infrastructure of western provinces bordering Central Asia, as part of the Western Development Program, officially launched in 1999.[15]

---

[13] See, for example, Nathan and Scobell, 2012; and David Shambaugh, *China Goes Global: The Partial Power*, Oxford, UK: Oxford University Press, 2013.

[14] This constitutes a remarkable reevaluation of the region's significance to China. Author interviews. See also Medeiros, 2009, p. 162.

[15] See Barry J. Naughton, "The Western Development Program," in Barry J. Naughton and Dali Yang, eds., *Holding China Together: Diversity and National Integration in the Post-Deng*

More recently, notably since 2010, Chinese leaders believe that they have perceived a more assertive U.S. effort to contain or constrain China.[16] This has been most strongly felt in the "near Seas" where China believes that the United States enjoys the preponderance of power with a strong network of alliances, notably Japan and South Korea, and where significant concentrations of American sea, air, and land power are located. Beijing also believes that the United States is strengthening its security relationship with India and enhancing ties with other security partners, including Australia and the Philippines.[17] From Beijing's vantage point, all this raises the question of how China should respond and break out of what looks like an encirclement strategy, a challenge that looks particularly daunting in East Asia.

It is in this context that some Chinese analysts have suggested that China should "march west" [*xijin*] because the U.S. encirclement strategy does not look as strong in Central Asia and beyond. As an April 2014 high-profile article in a prominent and authoritative CCP journal explains: "It is very difficult to become a powerful maritime state if [China] cannot break through the first and second island chains."[18] In China's far west, Washington does not have a network of alliances to block Beijing from breaking out; thus, China has greater opportunities to enhance its ties and expand its geopolitical and economic influence in Central Asia, the Middle East, and beyond.

Further west, North Atlantic Treaty Organization (NATO) member countries, located some distance away from China's borders, do not appear as hostile to Beijing as some U.S. allies in East Asia. But this does not mean that Beijing will concentrate on one geographic area

---

Era, New York: Cambridge University Press, 2004.

[16] Of course, other countries, including the United States, perceived China as becoming more assertive. For a discussion of these dueling perceptions, see, for example, Andrew Scobell and Scott W. Harold, "An 'Assertive' China? Insights from Interviews," *Asian Security*, Vol. 9, No. 2, 2013.

[17] For one analysis that emphasizes China's concern about Japan and India, see John W. Garver and Fei-ling Wang, "China's Anti Encirclement Struggle," *Asian Security*, Vol. 6, No. 3, September–December 2010.

[18] "Zhongguo 'xijin' yong pingheng zhanlue zhilu" ["China's 'March West' Guiding Balancing Strategy"], *Qiushi* [*Seeking Truth*], April 22, 2014.

at the expense of the other; indeed *xijin* is a "national security strategy for China to 'balance internally' by going both eastward and westward to counter daunting 'maritime geopolitical realities.'"[19]

The earliest and most widely publicized articulation of this proposal was by a prominent and highly respected academic. Peking University's Wang Jisi suggested in a widely read 2012 op-ed that China should pay more attention to its far west. Specifically, Wang advocated a more balanced geostrategic stance that gave consideration both to China's Central Asian hinterland and to the western Pacific.[20]

Silk Road and Strategic Partnerships

This proposal appeared to gain more traction in 2013, when Xi publicly declared the launch of several high-profile westward-directed initiatives, including the Silk Road Economic Belt and the Maritime Silk Road, purposefully invoking the name of the earliest trade route between China and the West via Central Asia and the Middle East. In a September 2013 speech focused on PRC policy toward Central Asia, delivered at a leading university in Kazakhstan, Xi articulated the idea of the New Silk Road and announced a number of new Chinese initiatives.[21] But this *xijin* approach should also be seen as a logical continuation or extension of China's strategy toward Central Asia in effect since the 1990s.[22]

Chinese analysts consider the Middle East a key global crossroads—an area of tremendous geostrategic importance—and Beijing think tanks are reportedly adding more Middle East analysts to their research staffs.[23] Together, the sizable oil reserves and the considerable invest-

---

[19] "Zhongguo 'xijin' yong pingheng zhanlue zhilu," 2014.

[20] See Wang Jisi, "'Xijin': Zhongguo diyuan zhanlue de zai pingheng" ["'Marching West': China's Geostrategic Rebalance"], *Huanqiu Shibao* [*Global Times*], October 17, 2012.

[21] See, for example, Wu Jiao and Zhang Yunbi, "Xi Proposes a 'New Silk Road' with Central Asia," *China Daily*, September 8, 2013.

[22] See, for example, Andrew Scobell, Ely Ratner, and Michael Beckley, *China's Strategy Toward Central and South Asia: An Empty Fortress*, Santa Monica, Calif.: RAND Corporation, RR-525-AF, 2014; and Kevin Sheives, "China Turns West: Beijing's Contemporary Strategy Towards Central Asia," *Pacific Affairs*, Vol. 79, No. 2, Summer 2006.

[23] Author interviews.

ment that China has reportedly made in the region suggest that the Middle East is only likely to grow even more important for Beijing in coming years. The region is also likely to remain significant as a market for Chinese goods and location for major infrastructure projects, and perhaps even as a source of capital investment in China.[24] Moreover, at least some Chinese analysts believe that Middle East states are likely to become "important political supporters" for China on the global stage.[25]

Two major Middle East powers of special interest to China are Saudi Arabia and Iran. Beijing has formed what it labeled "strategic partnerships" with Riyadh in 1999 and Tehran in 2000.[26] Saudi Arabia, a major oil exporter and one of the wealthiest states in the world (both in terms of total GDP and on a per capita basis) is an important player in the Middle East. While Riyadh is a key ally of Washington, it also enjoys close relations with Beijing. Iran is a major power in the region by a variety of measures. It is one of the most populous Middle East states, with 80 million people; only Egypt has more. And despite stringent sanctions, Iran continues to be one of the largest economies in the region. Tehran also has one of the region's most sizable and potent armed forces.

Indeed, China actively seeks out other powerful states that share its concerns about the perceived preponderance of global U.S. power.[27] Moreover, there are only a handful of such states that are both firmly outside the global U.S. network of allies and partners and possess sufficient power and determination to challenge U.S. policies. Iran, a major power in the Middle East, is also an intractable American adversary. Should China choose, Iran could potentially serve as an ally, helping the rising Asian power offset American influence in the Middle

---

[24] This is according to Chinese energy analysts and Middle East experts interviewed in early 2013. See Mathieu Duchatel, Oliver Brauner, and Zhou Hang, *Protecting China's Overseas Interests: The Slow Shift Away from Non-Interference*, SIPRI Policy Paper No. 41, Stockholm: Stockholm International Peace Research Institute, June 2014, p. 28. This point was also stressed in author interviews conducted in September 2014.

[25] See, for example, Li, 2004, p. 20.

[26] Medeiros, 2009, p. 163.

[27] For the logic as it refers to Iran, see Medeiros, 2009, p. 162.

East. But while China clearly sees the United States as a rival, Beijing does not seek to antagonize Washington unnecessarily. In fact, despite the strong undercurrent of great-power competition, China is keen to maintain cordial and cooperative relations with the United States, especially in the Middle East.[28] Beijing perceives Washington as a key provider of security in a region where no other power, including China, is capable of fulfilling this role. Therefore, China has been rather careful in its dealing with Iran, although rising U.S.-China tensions in East Asia could change China's constrained ties with Iran.

Internal and Peripheral Stability

China's third key interest in the Middle East is preserving internal security at home and around its periphery. CCP leaders fear domestic discontent.[29] According to one Chinese analyst: "The Middle East is a strategic extension of China's periphery." That analyst, Li Weijian, of the Shanghai Institutes of International Studies, explains:

> After the breakup of the Soviet Union, . . . a group of Islamic countries emerged in Central Asia, and it is an indisputable fact that the geopolitical distance between China and the Middle East shrank at once. China's western region was originally a neighbor of the Middle East and has long since been connected with the Middle East via the Silk Road; the two regions have close affinities and relations along ethnic, religious, and cultural dimensions. As the strategic extension of China's western border region, the trends governing the situation in the Middle East and the region's pan-nationalisms and extremist religious ideological trends have a direct influence on China's security and stability.[30]

The Middle East tugs at Beijing's insecurities with regard to popular dissent in the heavily populated "Han heartland," on China's fertile eastern plains and in coastal areas, as well as ethnic unrest in the

---

[28] Author interviews and author conversations.

[29] For studies that emphasis this point, see Susan Shirk, *China: Fragile Superpower*, Oxford, UK: Oxford University Press, 2007; and Nathan and Scobell, 2012.

[30] Li, 2014, pp. 18–19; RAND's translation.

more remote inland border regions inhabited by minority nationalities, such as Uighurs and Tibetans, who in recent years have displayed high levels of disaffection with Chinese control.[31]

The CCP worries that regional sympathy for the Uighurs may turn into vocal and material support for the Muslim Uighurs. Beijing works hard to discourage foreign support for what the CCP labels "terrorism, separatism and extremism" or "East Turkestan splittists."[32] China's greatest fear is that the Uighur struggle will become a global Muslim struggle similar to the 1980s war against Soviet occupation in Afghanistan.

In particular, Beijing fears the spread of radical Sunni Jihadi ideology among the Uighurs. Uighurs from China were captured in Afghanistan by coalition forces in the 2000s and interned in Guantanamo Bay. Moreover, Chinese Uighurs and Muslim Huis have reportedly joined so-called ISIL fighters in Syria and Iraq. As of late 2014, as many as 100 PRC citizens may have filled the ISIL ranks, along with disaffected Muslims from Europe and North America.[33]

Moreover, there was an uptick in terrorist attacks within China during 2013 and 2014. In October 2013, there was a dramatic incident in which an automobile careened into Beijing's Tiananmen Square and was set ablaze—the symbolic heart of China, and almost certainly the most heavily policed and closely monitored piece of real estate in China. A bomb exploded in Urumqi in April 2014, shortly after a visit to the city by Xi. Then, a month later, there was a deadly car bombing in the capital of the Xinjiang Uighur Autonomous Region. There have been other incidents—notably, two shocking knife attacks in crowded southern Chinese train stations, involving multiple assailants (Kunming, Yunnan Province, in March 2014 and Guangzhou, Guangdong Province, in May 2014). Both episodes have been blamed on Uighur

---

[31] Li, 2014, pp. 18–19.

[32] Chu and Jin, 2008, p. 264. See also Medeiros, 2009, p. 166.

[33] Author interviews and "Chinese Militants Get Islamic State 'Terrorist Training': Media," Reuters, September 22, 2014. However, the percentage of non-Arab fighters in ISIL forces appears to very small—approximately 10 percent. Personal communication from Jon Alterman.

extremists.[34] As the U.S. military drawdowns in Afghanistan approach China is fearful about what this will mean for its interests in the Xinjiang Uighur Autonomous Region.[35]

Chinese analysts acknowledge that what is perceived to be the plight of a downtrodden ethnic group in western China finds sympathy within the Middle East.[36] Thus, Beijing does everything possible to quash expressions of public or official support from any foreign country for the PRC Uighurs. To date China has been successful in its goal. A notable exception was the Turkish government's condemnation of the 2009 Chinese crackdown on ethnic unrest in Xinjiang.[37]

In addition, Chinese leaders are concerned about the demonstration effect of the Arab Spring, which began in Tunisia in 2011, before toppling dictatorial regimes in Libya and Egypt. The Arab Spring rekindled CCP fears of political unrest inside the majority-ethnic Han heartland of China.[38] Beijing was alarmed at the specter of the Jasmine Revolution, triggered by the demonstration effect of the wave of Middle East uprisings. More than 25 years after the 1989 Chinese democracy movement, Chinese leaders are sensitive to the prospect of urban unrest.[39] This worry has only increased with the emergence of the Umbrella Movement in Hong Kong in late 2014.

Great-Power Status

China's fourth major interest in the Middle East is to enhance Beijing's status as a great power. For China's leaders, national security begins at

---

[34] Barbara Demick, "Xinjiang Attacks Attributed to China's Uighurs Grow in Sophistication," *Los Angeles Times*, May 22, 2014.

[35] Andrew Scobell, "China Ponders Post-2014 Afghanistan: Neither 'All in' nor Bystander," *Asian Survey*, Vol. 55, No. 2, March–April 2015.

[36] See, for example, Niu, 2014a, p. 40.

[37] Niu, 2014a, p. 41.

[38] Some Chinese analysts allude to this issue. One writer noted that the "lost legitimacy" of Mubarak, Gaddafi, and Assad made Beijing uneasy and prompted fears of the "infiltration of Western ideologies." Niu, 2014a, p. 42.

[39] Andrew Jacobs, "Tiananmen Square Anniversary Prompts Campaign of Silence," *New York Times*, May 28, 2014.

home and is conflated with regime security—Beijing's paramount security concern is ensuring the continued rule of the CCP.[40] This means retaining political legitimacy in the eyes of the Chinese people and maintaining firm political control based on the CCP being perceived as a staunch champion of China's interests. It may seem paradoxical that a dictatorial regime would pay such close attention to public opinion, but the CCP attaches great importance to its image in the eyes of the Chinese people.[41] Because of China's growing economic, military, and diplomatic clout in the era of reform, the Chinese people increasingly expect to see their country playing diplomatic and even military roles in key international issues and major hot spots.

Therefore, in 2003, Beijing insisted on staking out a "principled" and independent position on U.S. intervention in Iraq. Beijing also took a position toward the Syrian civil war at variance with U.S. policy, urging that "the current crisis . . . be resolved through political dialogue in a peaceful manner,"[42] rather than through the overthrow of Assad's regime. To maintain influence in the Middle East, China seeks to avoid antagonizing existing governments—emphasizing its principle of noninterference and support for stability. According to one analyst: "China has never queried the legitimacy of Middle East governments, but that puts it in a dilemma when governments are facing fierce opposition from their people."[43]

Furthermore, for many decades, Beijing has claimed the mantle of leadership of the developing world and identifies itself as a developing or "third world" country. This is important because China views itself as very different from developed countries, Western powers, and superpowers past and present. Unlike those states, China does not perceive itself as an imperialist power, and China believes that it has no history of oppressing non-Western countries; it also does not currently seek to exploit developing states. Beijing insists that it has no hege-

---

[40] Nathan and Scobell, 2012.

[41] Author interviews.

[42] "China Issues 6-Point Statement on Syria," CCTV.com, March 4. 2012.

[43] Niu, 2014a, pp. 42–43.

monic ambitions, unlike the former Soviet Union or the United States, and sides with the developing world.[44] Since the early 1950s, Beijing has insisted that its relations with developing states were guided by the Five Principles of Peaceful Coexistence—namely, mutual respect for territorial integrity and sovereignty, nonaggression, noninterference in internal affairs, equality and mutual benefit, and peaceful coexistence.[45] This was the position China staked out at the 1955 Asian-African Conference of nonaligned states, held in Bandung, Indonesia. Then, in 1974, during a major speech delivered to the United Nations General Assembly, Deng Xiaoping proclaimed that China was part of a "third world"—in contrast to a U.S.-led capitalist bloc of "first world" states and a Soviet-led socialist bloc of "second world."

These principles of peaceful coexistence were to a considerable extent maintained during the first four decades of PRC foreign policy, when Beijing had limited involvement, presence, or interests in the developing world. However, since the 1990s, as China has become increasingly involved in the developing world, the Five Principles of Peaceful Coexistence have proved far more challenging for Beijing to uphold.[46]

Growing numbers of PRC citizens expect their government to behave similarly to the governments of other great powers and take steps to protect China's greater overseas interests, not just in the Asia-Pacific region but in the wider world. Some Chinese analysts argue that China's expanding interests in the Middle East—especially safeguarding Chinese nationals and countering threats to China's energy

[44] Peter Van Ness, "China as a Third World State: Foreign Policy and Official National Identity," in Lowell Dittmer and Samuel S. Kim, eds., *China's Quest for National Identity*, Ithaca, N.Y.: Cornell University Press, 1993.

[45] Steven I. Levine, "China in Asia: The PRC as a Regional Power," in Harry Harding, ed., *China's Foreign Relations in the 1980s*, New Haven, Conn.: Yale University Press, 1984, pp. 116–117.

[46] See, for example, Yitzhak Shichor, "Fundamentally Unacceptable yet Occasionally Unavoidable: China's Options on External Interference in the Middle East," *China Report*, Vol. 49, No. 1, 2013.

security—demand a more "proactive response," including the possible use of military force.[47]

In recent years, protecting Chinese nationals overseas has become a priority, and an issue that Beijing feels vulnerability on when it comes to domestic criticism. The safety of Chinese citizens abroad is a key component of China's overseas interests—an increasingly noteworthy type of national interest. Indeed, it was highlighted in a speech by Hu Jintao at the 18th CCP Congress, in November 2012. There are reportedly no precise or official PRC statistics on the number of Chinese citizens living abroad. But analysts estimate that approximately 5 million Chinese reside beyond the country's borders, with an estimated 550,000 located in the Middle East.[48] Today's Chinese expats have greater expectations than previous generations and expect their government to respond if their safety is threatened. Moreover, Chinese citizens have ready access to cell phones and the Internet and could use them to publicize their plight. One recent report on China's overseas interests highlights that the "protection of nationals abroad is much more likely to lead . . . toward greater intervention than the protection of energy interests."[49]

Beijing's desire to be seen as a great power both by other states and by the Chinese people has also led to greater Chinese military involvement in the Middle East during the past several decades. The willingness and capability to employ military forces in the region marks a dramatic departure from earlier positions, in which China refused to get involved directly in regional problems. Some noteworthy examples of greater Chinese military involvement in the past 30 years in the Middle East and North Africa include participation in United Nations peacekeeping operations, participation in antipiracy efforts, and the

---

[47] Qian Xuewen, "Zhong Dong jubian dui Zhongguo haiwai liyi de yingxiang" ["Impact of Middle East Turmoil on China's Overseas Interests"], *Alabo Shijie Yanjiu* [*Arab World Studies*], No. 6, November 2012. See also Zhao Jingfang, "Pojie nengyuan anquan kunjing: waijiao he junshi shouduan" ["Solving Energy Difficulties: Diplomatic and Military Methods"], *Shijie Zhishi* [*World Affairs*], No. 18, 2012, pp. 50–51. Zhao is a professor at the People's Liberation Army (PLA) National Defense University.

[48] Niu, 2014a, pp. 41–42.

[49] Duchatel, Brauner, and Zhou, 2014, p. 50.

noncombatant evacuation of Chinese citizens. Each of these indicated a greater Chinese willingness to play a more active role in the Middle East and North Africa.

China's first involvement was in 1990, when five military observers were dispatched to the United Nations Truce Supervision Organization in the Golan Heights. As of December 2012, China had 335 engineering and medical personnel for the United Nations Interim Force in Lebanon and hundreds of personnel under United Nations auspices in Sudan.[50] Beijing's decision in December 2008 to dispatch a three-ship PLA Navy flotilla to engage in antipiracy operations in the Gulf of Aden was another dramatic break with the past.[51] Then, in 2011, for the first time, PLA air and naval units played a key but very limited role in the evacuation of more than 35,000 Chinese citizens via air and sea from Libya. The military assets just happened to be in the region, but the driving force was the rising popular expectations for the CCP to act decisively in protecting Chinese citizens at risk halfway around the world. Other evacuations of Chinese citizens have been conducted in Lebanon in 2006, Egypt in 2011, Syria in 2011 and 2013, and Yemen in 2015, all organized by PRC civilian ministries, including the Ministry of Foreign Affairs, but none of these—except Yemen—had full PLA involvement.[52]

---

[50] International Crisis Group, *China's Growing Role in UN Peacekeeping*, Asia Report No. 166, Brussels, April 17, 2009; and Bates Gill and Chin-hao Huang, "China's Expanding Presence in UN Peacekeeping Operations and Implications for the United States," in Roy Kamphausen, David Lai, and Andrew Scobell, eds., *Beyond the Strait: PLA Missions Other Than Taiwan*, Carlisle Barracks, Pa.: U.S. Army War College Strategic Studies Institute, 2009. See also Information Office of the State Council, *The Diversified Employment of China's Armed Forces*, Beijing, April 2013.

[51] Andrew S. Erickson and Austin M. Strange, *No Substitute for Experience: Chinese Antipiracy Operations in the Gulf of Aden*, China Maritime Study No. 10, Newport, R.I.: U.S. Naval War College, November 2013.

[52] For a concise summary and analysis of the Libyan Noncombatant Evacuation Operation (NEO), see Duchatel, Brauner, and Zhou, 2014, pp. 48–50. For summary of the Yemeni NEO, see Shannon Tiezzi, "Chinese Nationals Evacuate Yemen on PLA Navy Frigate," *The Diplomat*, March 30, 2015.

Conclusion

The Middle East has become increasingly important to Beijing since the early 1990s, as rising Chinese energy demand and growing economic stakes have combined with enduring geostrategic interests. As China's national interests in the region have expanded, Beijing appears to have formulated a discernible wary-dragon strategy—whereby China is reluctant to increase its security involvement or raise its diplomatic profile—although it remains officially unarticulated. In short, China feels vulnerable in the Middle East but is uncertain about how to protect its growing interests in the region. The following Chinese interests in the Middle East and corresponding national objectives have been identified in this chapter. Energy security and economic stakes seem to be Beijing's paramount interest, and Beijing's objective here appears to be securing access to resources and markets in the region. Xi's formal launching of the New Silk Road initiative underscores economics as China's top priority.

China's second most important interest is its geostrategic posture in the region. Beijing seeks to balance against U.S. influence in the Middle East, but this does not mean that Beijing actively desires to oppose Washington or significantly expand its military footprint. Rather, China seeks to cooperate with the United States because Beijing considers Washington a critical force for stability in the region, although the two capitals disagree on their definitions of what conditions are conducive to stability. China's third key interest in the Middle East is ensuring domestic tranquility back home. The primary objective here is to quash any public criticism of Chinese policies, notably with regard to Chinese Muslims and the Uighurs of Xinjiang. Beijing is especially vigilant in quietly lobbying to ensure that no Middle East government expresses official support for Uighurs in the PRC or permits public criticism of Chinese policies or actions toward the Uighurs. Beijing's fourth and final key interest in the Middle East is the enhancement China's great-power status. To this end, China's goal is to receive respect and diplomatic deference befitting a great power from the countries of the region.

A first cut at assessing China's Middle East strategy suggests that it has been quite successful to date, at least based on how well Beijing has been able to protect the four key interests and promote its related objectives identified. But this is only a preliminary assessment. A more thorough judgment requires a closer look to assess how exactly China is protecting these interests and promoting these objectives in specific cases. The following two chapters focus on the instruments and mechanisms that China is employing in its relationships with two key Middle East powers: Saudi Arabia and Iran.

CHAPTER THREE

China Engages Saudi Arabia

This chapter and the following chapter focus on China's management of bilateral relations with key states in the region. This chapter examines how Beijing employs the instruments of national power to promote its interests and advance its objectives in Saudi Arabia and the wider Middle East. China and Saudi Arabia have vigorous and growing ties. Bilateral relations have expanded significantly during the past quarter century. One U.S. analyst, writing in 2012, opined that bilateral economic ties have become both "wide and deep."[1]

Chapter Two identified PRC interests and objectives for the Middle East. To recapitulate, these are (1) securing access to energy resources and thriving economic relationships; (2) balancing against the United States but seeking cooperation; (3) quashing morale or material support for Muslim extremists in the PRC; and (4) receiving the respect befitting a great power. This chapter analyzes China's relations with the Kingdom of Saudi Arabia. This approach can provide a useful way to evaluate the extent to which China has or has not been implementing its wary-dragon strategy successfully both before and after the establishment of full diplomatic relations between Beijing and Riyadh in 1990. A review of diplomatic, economic, and military realms suggests that Beijing has been very successful in implementing its Middle East strategy.

---

[1] Thomas W. Lippman, *Saudi Arabia on the Edge: The Uncertain Future*, Washington, D.C.: Potomac Books, 2013, p. 256.

Chinese Instruments and Mechanisms

China's strategy toward Saudi Arabia can be divided into two eras: before and after 1990, the year the two states established full diplomatic relations (after Riyadh had broken off official ties with Taipei). Pre-1990, China's primary instruments were diplomatic and military, and its goals were geostrategic and oriented toward great-power status. Beijing was a latecomer to the Middle East and was playing catch-up with the two superpowers. Moreover, the PRC was focused on strengthening its claim to be the sole legitimate government of China and was engaged in a struggle to persuade states—including Saudi Arabia, with continued ambassador-level diplomatic relations with the ROC on Taiwan—to switch recognition from Taipei to Beijing. China was not a major player in the Middle East prior to the 1990s, and to increase its influence in the region, Beijing looked for any leverage. What Beijing found was military, in the form of the sale of ballistic missiles—a weapon system no other major power was willing to provide to Riyadh. This deal helped pave the way for the normalization of relations in 1990. Following this geostrategic breakthrough, China has emphasized economic ties, although it has not neglected diplomatic and military elements, to advance its interests in Saudi Arabia.

Diplomacy: Geostrategic Success and Rising Great-Power Status

Pre-1990 Era

Beijing first entered the Middle East as a diplomatic player in the 1970s. Upon admission into the United Nations in 1971, the PRC replaced the ROC (Taiwan) and assumed its permanent seat on the Security Council. And following President Richard Nixon's historic trip to Beijing a year later, and the eventual full normalization of U.S.-Chinese relations in 1979, China's global stature grew appreciably. Nevertheless, many states in the region, including Saudi Arabia, maintained full diplomatic relations with Taiwan. Therefore, the diplomatic rivalry with Taipei was a major motivation for Beijing while expanding its influence in the Middle East. A sustained struggle ensued to persuade capitals across the region to sever ties with Taipei. The PRC made slow diplomatic progress in the Middle East—an area of the world where the two Cold War superpowers dominated and China remained largely an outsider.

The Middle East faced great instability in the 1980s. Saudi Arabia felt threatened by Iran's revolutionary Islamic regime, which was engaged in a brutal war with Iraq, and the continued specter of Soviet-sponsored communism loomed over the region. Riyadh, located in an unstable neighborhood and facing multiple threats and challenges, sought to strengthen its defense capabilities. The Saudis tried to acquire advanced jet fighters and other conventional weaponry from their main ally, the United States.

When this effort was stymied by opposition from Israel, Saudi Arabia found another country—China—that was willing to provide a significant new capability: intermediate-range ballistic missiles (IRBMs). China was willing to provide IRBMs to Saudi Arabia in the mid-1980s for two major reasons: the financial compensation was substantial and the sale allowed Beijing to gain political influence in a key Middle East capital allied with the United States.[2] The sale and delivery of the IRBMs was conducted in secret, but when news of it became public, it created tremendous controversy. The missiles were capable of hitting targets in a wide array of countries in the region, including Israel.

Within a few years, the global power configuration appeared to be shifting significantly. The events of 1989 signaled the waning of Soviet power, and the fall of the Berlin Wall heralded the unraveling of the Soviet bloc. The Soviet collapse in 1991 left Saudi Arabia with a very powerful U.S. patron, the sole remaining superpower. China was also viewed as the world's most dynamic rising power with a growing presence in the Middle East.

For Riyadh, this meant a higher priority for its relations with Beijing. Rapprochement was made easier by the belief that China, while a communist regime, was not militarily or ideologically threatening (unlike the Soviet Union) and at the same time offered the possibility

[2] On the motives driving PRC arms exports, see the discussion in John W. Lewis, Hua Di, and Xue Litai, "Beijing's Defense Establishment: Solving The Arms-Export Enigma," *International Security*, Vol. 15, No. 4, Spring 1991.

of economic and even security cooperation. Moreover, Riyadh could appreciate Beijing's overriding desire to maintain domestic stability, no matter the cost. In the aftermath of the June 1989 massacre in Tiananmen Square, while many countries around the world worked to distance themselves from the PRC, Riyadh was prepared to move forward and negotiate the establishment of full diplomatic relations. After signing a memorandum of understanding agreeing to the opening of trade offices in November 1988, the PRC and Saudi Arabia moved swiftly to establish full diplomatic relations in July 1990, despite the events in Tiananmen Square.[3]

Post-1990 Era

Within a few years, China's economy had rebounded from the post-Tiananmen slump as paramount leader Deng Xiaoping successfully reinvigorated Beijing's policy of reform and opening to the outside world. As a result, domestic production could not meet China's dramatically increasing thirst for energy. By 1993, China had become a net importer of oil. Major oil producers, such as Saudi Arabia, became more important to China, and the Middle East grew into a much more geostrategic region of the world. Beijing had a far greater interest in increasing its influence and in maintaining Middle East stability, which directly affected China's energy and economic security.

In contrast to the increasing involvement by Beijing, Riyadh became concerned about what it perceived to be a drop in Washington's level of commitment to the region. Indicators of this alleged declining commitment by Washington include the U.S. occupation (2003) and then military withdrawal (2012) from Iraq, its troop drawdown in Afghanistan, the Obama administration's hosting of a Muslim Brotherhood delegation in Washington (early 2015), and declining U.S. oil imports from the kingdom. Moreover, Saudi Arabia became increasingly unhappy with Washington's overall policy conduct, including its lack of military intervention in Syria, negotiations with Iran over the nuclear program, and U.S. advocacy for democratization in the Middle

[3] "China and Saudi Arabia" website of the PRC Embassy in Jeddah, August 26, 2004.

East. Together these issues raised doubts in Riyadh regarding Washington's long-term reliability as an ally.[4]

Symbolism can be as important as substance in international relations. Visits by senior U.S. political leaders can send powerful signals about the value of a bilateral relationship. This is especially true in the Middle East, when more outside powers pay greater attention to the region, and this is manifest in a higher volume of trips by senior leaders from such countries as Japan, South Korea, and China.[5] In terms of high-level visits—and security cooperation, including arms sales—U.S.-Saudi ties seem quite robust (see Figure 3.1).[6] The most recent visit by President Barack Obama was in January 2015, after the death of King Abdullah. This was his third visit to the kingdom as head of state (the first occurred in June 2009). But Obama's visit was because of increasing tensions between Washington and Riyadh and was aimed at reassuring Saudi leaders that the United States was still vigorously committed to its partnership with Saudi Arabia.[7] The decision by King Salman Bin Abdul Aziz not to attend the summit between the United States and the Gulf Cooperation Council (GCC), held May 2015 in Washington, was taken as a Saudi snub to signal displeasure at the Obama administration's efforts to follow through on a

[4] These concerns are voiced by Saudi officials, privately and not so privately. See, for example, Martin Chulov, "Barack Obama Arrives in Saudi Arabia for Brief Visit with Upset Arab Ally," *Guardian*, March 28, 2014; and "Saudi Arabia and the United States: Awkward Relations," *The Economist*, March 29, 2014, p. 47. These concerns have also been noted by Chinese analysts. See, for example, Li, 2014, pp. 28–30.

[5] Christopher Davidson, *The Persian Gulf and Pacific Asia: From Indifference to Interdependence*, New York: Columbia University Press, 2010, pp. 79–94.

[6] We coded Chinese high-level visits as those by the President, Vice President, Premier, State Councilors, Politburo Standing Committee and Politburo members, Chairman of the National People's Congress, Chairman of the Chinese People's Political Consultative Conference, the Foreign Minister, the Defense Minister, the Minister of Public Security, special envoys, and a trip by the head of Sinopec. We coded U.S. high-level visits as those by the President, Vice President, the Secretary of State, the Secretary of Defense, the Chairman of the Joint Chiefs of Staff, the CIA Director, the Speaker of the House, and special envoys.

[7] Chulov, 2014.

Figure 3.1
High-Level Chinese and U.S. Visits to Saudi Arabia, 1990–2014

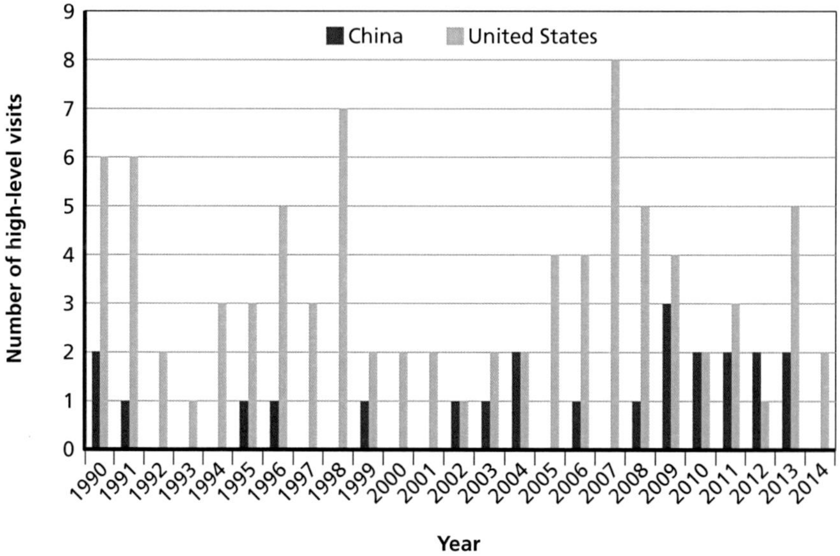

SOURCE: Compiled by authors from RAND databases.
RAND *RR1229-3.1*

nuclear deal with Iran.[8] However, Salman's ascension to the throne of the House of Saud following the death of Abdullah in January 2015 is not expected to disrupt the close and enduring ties between Riyadh and Washington.[9]

For Saudi Arabia, China may present a partial solution to its uneasy partnership with the United States. China is a large, economically dynamic, ideologically moderate, and politically stable country that does not focus on human rights and imposes little, if any, restrictions on the kinds of weapon systems Saudi Arabia could purchase. Furthermore, Beijing has been actively wooing Riyadh with increased

[8] Helene Cooper, "Saudi Arabia Says King Won't Attend Meetings in U.S.," *New York Times*, May 10, 2015.

[9] Frederic Wehrey, "After King Abdullah, Continuity," Carnegie Endowment for International Peace, January 23, 2015.

numbers of visits by senior Chinese leaders since the mid-2000s (see Figure 3.1), including two visits by PRC President Hu Jintao—one in 2006 and another in 2009.[10]

In a matter of a few short decades, Beijing and Riyadh have established the foundation for an enduring relationship. Senior Chinese leaders have traveled to Saudi Arabia since the two countries established ambassador-level relations, in 1990 (see Figure 3.1). Among these were head-of-state visits, including one by President Jiang Zemin, in 1999, which produced a bilateral agreement to expand energy cooperation. Then, in January 2006, King Abdullah traveled to China for his first state trip abroad since assuming the Saudi throne.[11] Just three months later, in April 2006, Hu Jintao visited Saudi Arabia and signed agreements on energy and security cooperation. The PRC president became only the second foreign leader to address the Saudi legislative council. And Hu paid a second visit to Saudi Arabia in February 2009, where he stressed that "China attaches great importance to bilateral relations with Saudi Arabia" and emphasized that Beijing was keen to "deepen pragmatic cooperation" between the two countries.[12] The relationship also has religious and philanthropic dimensions. The latter was evident when the Saudi government made the largest foreign donation of any country to the victims of the 2008 Sichuan earthquake.[13]

It is clear that the newest generation of Chinese leaders continue to place high value on Beijing's relationship with Riyadh. PRC President Xi rose to become China's paramount leader by March 2013 and is expected to serve in this position until 2023. In March 2014, Xi told visiting Saudi Arabian Deputy Prime Minister (and concurrently defense minister) Crown Prince Salman Bin-Abdul Aziz Al Saud (and

---

[10] In addition, Hu's predecessor, Jiang Zemin, paid a visit to Saudi Arabia in 1999.

[11] Karen Elliott House, *On Saudi Arabia: Its People, Past, Religion, Fault Lines—and Future*, New York: Knopf, 2012, p. 238.

[12] "Chinese President Arrives in Riyadh at Start of 'Trip of Friendship, Cooperation,'" *Xinhua*, February 10, 2009.

[13] The Saudi government reportedly provided 27.5 million U.S. dollars in financial assistance and 5.5 million U.S. dollars in supplies. "Chinese President Arrives in Riyadh at Start of 'Trip of Friendship, Cooperation,'" 2009.

king since January 2015): "Both sides should take energy cooperation as a pillar and expand partnership in aerospace and new energy to forge closer ties."[14] The Chinese leader invited Riyadh to join Beijing's Silk Road Economic Belt and Maritime Silk Road. Xi emphasized that Saudi Arabia was "China's good friend, brother, and partner in the Middle East and Gulf region." Xi also made a point of expressing "China's support to Saudi Arabia for choosing a development path that suits its own conditions."[15] This comment is Beijing's way of signaling that China pursues a policy of noninterference, and, unlike the United States, it does not lecture Saudi Arabia about human rights or internal repression.

Washington might not pay close attention to the number of times senior officials visit a region or country, but other countries do. Visits by national-level leaders are seen as indicators of the degree of value a state attaches to its relationship with another state. China in particular is prone to such metrics, especially because symbolism and ceremony are considered as important as substance. Moreover, high-level visits also tend to produce deliverables. Therefore, these visits are useful gauges of the level of commitment of one country to another.[16]

An examination of the frequency of visits by PRC high-level officials to Saudi Arabia since the normalization of relations in 1990 reveals an intermittent but continual flow of senior leaders to Riyadh. Moreover, in the late 2000s, there was a noticeable uptick in such visits, underscoring the growing importance that China attaches to Saudi Arabia. While high-level U.S. officials have visited the kingdom with greater annual frequency than their Chinese counterparts over the past two decades, there has been an increase in visits by PRC officials. The frequency of these annual visits began to approach those by U.S. officials during the six-year period from 2008 to 2013, although the U.S. frequency remained noticeably higher—2.8 per year for U.S. officials compared with 2.0 for PRC officials. However, almost three years into Xi's tenure as PRC president, he has yet to visit Saudi Arabia,

---

[14] Shannon Tiezzi, "Saudi Arabia, China's Good Friend," *The Diplomat*, March 14, 2014a.

[15] Tiezzi, 2014a.

[16] Davidson, 2010, p. 79.

which suggests that Beijing's relationship with Riyadh has become complicated for China. The Silk Road project is Xi's flagship foreign policy initiative, and the Middle East is a key regional component of this effort. Under these circumstances, one would expect that a visit to China's most important energy source in the region would be a high priority for Xi during his first presidential term. However, consistent with Beijing's wary-dragon strategy, China exhibits great caution and extreme reluctance, fearful of upsetting its delicate diplomatic balancing act in the Middle East.

Sensitive Bilateral Issues

China is engaged in a sustained and ongoing effort to sidestep controversy, preempt public disagreements, and silence criticism. Beijing exerts considerable pressure on other states to not express openly public condemnation or even concern over China's internal affairs. For Middle Eastern or Muslim states, the taboo topics tend to be Beijing's treatment of Muslims, particularly Uighurs. But other topics are also important—such as support for one China and national unity, which means not expressing any views that could be construed as supporting or sympathizing with the dilemmas of Taiwan, Tibet, or Xinjiang.

An important international and domestic symbol of Beijing's commitment to the fair treatment of Islam is support for the hajj. Since 1955, the PRC has annually permitted Chinese Muslims to make pilgrimages to Saudi Arabia (with a 15-year hiatus between 1964 and 1979). For Beijing, this flow helps legitimize the regime in the eyes of approximately 20 million Chinese Muslims. Moreover, it offers a way for Beijing to reward loyal, moderate Chinese Muslims. At the same time, it provides clear evidence to the Saudis and other Muslim states that China respects the religious beliefs and practices of its people. It presents a kinder, gentler face to balance the brutal image of Chinese repression in Xinjiang.[17] The annual number of hajj sojourners from China to Mecca held steady at 6,000 during the 1990s, but by 2003

[17] Ben Simpfendorfer, *The New Silk Road: How a Rising Arab World Is Turning Away from the West and Rediscovering China*, Basingstoke, UK: Palgrave Macmillan, 2009, pp. 171–172.

the flow had reportedly risen to more than 10,000.[18] The majority of these PRC citizens appear to be Hui Muslims rather than Uighurs or other ethnic minorities. Hui are virtually indistinguishable from ethnic Han Chinese, are geographically dispersed throughout China, and are culturally assimilated, whereas Uighurs are a Turkic people racially and culturally distinct from the Han and are mostly concentrated in western China's Xinjiang Uighur Autonomous Region. The former tend to be considered more reliable and far less susceptible to the three evils of "terrorism, separatism, and extremism."[19]

Moreover, China has managed to successfully avoid taking clear-cut stands on controversial issues and has brushed over differences in Middle East affairs. Two key issues have proved particularly problematic for closer Sino-Saudi relations: Syria and Iran. Riyadh and Beijing have similar views on the Arab Spring—both view the popular movements across the Arab world as threatening—but they have differed in their approaches to the Syrian civil war. China defers to Russia and tends to oppose foreign intervention or "meddling" in Syria, while Saudi Arabia tends to support foreign, particularly U.S. or Western, military intervention. Riyadh wants to topple the Assad regime, which is backed by Iran, Saudi Arabia's greatest rival in the Middle East.[20] Beijing has little in the way of concrete national interests in Damascus, unlike Moscow, which has had close ties with the Assad regime and significant numbers of Russian citizens living in Syria—mostly Russian women married to local men.[21]

For China, the important issue at stake in Syria is the international legal principle of state sovereignty and the PRC's long-held prin-

---

[18] John Calabrese, "Saudi Arabia and China Extend Ties Beyond Oil," *China Brief*, Vol. 5, No. 20, October 2005.

[19] Brent Crane, "A Tale of Two Chinese Muslim Minorities," *The Diplomat*, August 22, 2014.

[20] Jasper Wong, "Saudi-China Relations Emblematic of China's New Foreign Policy Challenges," *The Interpreter*, July 18, 2014.

[21] One Chinese Middle East expert said: "We [Chinese] really don't have any interests in Syria." Author interviews.

ciple of noninterference in the internal affairs of other states.[22] Finally, China is extremely reluctant to support intervention in Syria after feeling betrayed in Libya in 2011. Beijing supported the United Nations Security Council's Resolution 1970 (which imposed an arms embargo, among other things). A month later, China abstained on Resolution 1973, which imposed a no-fly zone over Libya. In Beijing's view, the shift to more-active NATO air support for the opposition "exceeded the mandate."[23] China believed that it was agreeing to a restrained, defensive policy, not a vigorous, offensive-oriented air operation.

China and Saudi Arabia also differ on Iran. Whereas Beijing views Tehran as an enduring, albeit difficult, friend (see Chapter Four), Riyadh sees Tehran as its major rival and adversary in the region. Thus, Iran is the key issue for Saudi Arabia, and the Syrian civil war is a subsidiary issue.[24] According to Wu Bingbing of Peking University, one of the "internal contradictions" in Beijing's approach to the Persian Gulf has been "the competition or . . . antagonism between Saudi Arabia and Iran since the 1979 Islamic Revolution."[25] The PRC's relationship with Iran dates back to the 1970s, and the two countries remain close, even if their ties have become complicated (see Chapter Four). Since both Tehran and Riyadh view each other with great suspicion and as rivals, the fact that China enjoys friendly ties with Iran is a source of friction.

Nevertheless, there is significant public criticism of China in Saudi "elitist" and "populist" media outlets on the topics of Syria and Xinjiang. Over the years, public views of China in Saudi Arabia have been mixed—a combination of positive and negative perspectives. On the one hand, many Saudis exhibit "clear admiration for the Chinese

[22] Chu Shulong, "Bei Fei Zhong Dong jushi yu Zhongguo" ["China and the Changing Situation in the Middle East and North Africa"], *Xiandai Guoji Guanxi* [*Contemporary International Relations*], No. 3, 2011.

[23] Duchatel, Brauner, and Zhou, 2014, p. 11.

[24] Personal communication to the authors from Jon Alterman.

[25] Wu Bingbing, "Strategy and Politics in the Gulf as Seen from China," in Bryce Wakefield and Susan L. Levenstein, eds., *China and the Persian Gulf: Implications for the United States*, Washington, D.C.: Woodrow Wilson International Center for Scholars, 2011, p. 22.

model of [economic] development and its perceived ability to wed its traditional culture with modernity."[26] On the other hand, many Saudis have "genuine fears about . . . [China's] treatment of local Muslims . . . [and China's] identity as a country . . . [of] 'state atheism.'"[27] But since at least the early years of the 21st century, there have been "large negative pluralities" toward China in Saudi public opinion. In contrast to the "intensifying political and economic engagement between Saudi Arabia and China," there has been "a sustained negative perception about China among the wider Saudi public."[28] A "major turning point" in Saudi perceptions of China was the July 2009 riots in Xinjiang, which many Saudis viewed as Chinese brutality against Muslims.[29] Then, "[s]ince the first UN Security Council vote in October of 2011, the Saudi media has maintained a largely negative tone in its coverage of China's role in the Syrian crisis."[30]

Energy and Economic Cooperation

The PRC looms ever larger as a Saudi energy and economic partner, while the United States seems to diminish in importance in this respect. According to one U.S. expert: "Whereas U.S. oil demand is stagnant, Chinese oil demand is growing strongly and is projected to continue to do so."[31] Moreover, Beijing prefers Riyadh over Tehran as an "energy partner" because Saudi Arabia is considered a less truculent and more

---

[26] Mohammend Turki Al-Sudairi, *China in the Eyes of the Saudi Media*, GRC Gulf Papers, Jeddah, Saudi Arabia: Gulf Research Center, February 2013, p. 9. "Elitist" newspapers are those read by the elite, and "populist" are those read by ordinary Saudis. According to Al-Sudairi, "All Saudi newspapers . . . reflect the official line on some level . . . due to the nature of censorship." However, populist papers are given "more leeway in their censorship."

[27] Al-Sudairi, 2013, p. 31.

[28] Al-Sudairi, 2013, p. 6.

[29] Al-Sudairi, 2013, p. 14.

[30] Al-Sudairi, 2013, p. 20.

[31] Jon B. Alterman, "The Vital Triangle," in Bryce Wakefield and Susan L. Levenstein, eds., *China and the Persian Gulf: Implications for the United States*, Washington, D.C.: Woodrow Wilson International Center for Scholars, 2011, p. 28.

reliable oil supplier.[32] Since 2002, Saudi Arabia has been China's top source of imported crude oil, and Riyadh has given Beijing repeated assurances—given at the highest levels, most notably during President Hu's visit to Riyadh in February 2009—that China can count on the kingdom to provide a steady supply of crude oil.[33] A senior Chinese diplomat and former ambassador to Riyadh publicly stated just prior to Hu's visit that petroleum cooperation between China and Saudi Arabia would likely endure for 50 years.[34]

An official Chinese domestic news agency commentary released in January 2006 concisely captures the value of Saudi Arabia in China's eyes: "Saudi Arabia is a very good and reliable oil supplier. It is not like Nigeria, which is so fraught with uncertain factors that its oil supply fluctuates sharply. Neither is it like Iraq and Iran, whose oil supply was affected by unstable political situations."[35]

Saudi Aramco's president and CEO told reporters in 2010: "Demographic and economic trends are making it clear—the writing is on the wall. China is the growth market for petroleum."[36] Chinese demand for petroleum (and other energy resources) is increasing while U.S. demand is flat, and European demand is also flat.[37] Indeed, China has grown more reliant on Saudi Arabia for oil. Chinese imports of Saudi petroleum have risen from a negligible amount in 1998 to almost 1.1 million barrels per day by 2013. By contrast, U.S. reliance on Saudi oil has declined: from 1.5 million barrels per day to 1.3 million barrels

---

[32] Jean-Francois Seznec, "China and the Gulf in 2010: A Political Economic Survey," in Bryce Wakefield and Susan L. Levenstein, eds., *China and the Persian Gulf: Implications for the United States*, Washington, D.C.: Woodrow Wilson International Center for Scholars, 2011, p. 56.

[33] Erica Downs, "China-Gulf Energy Relations," in Bryce Wakefield and Susan L. Levenstein, eds., *China and the Persian Gulf: Implications for the United States*, Washington, D.C.: Woodrow Wilson International Center for Scholars, 2011, pp. 62–63.

[34] Downs, 2011, p. 66.

[35] *Zhongguo Tongxunshe*, January 20, 2006, as quoted in Alterman and Garver, 2008, p. 33.

[36] Jad Mouawad, "China's Growth Shifts the Geopolitics of Oil," *New York Times,* March 19, 2010.

[37] Personal communication to authors from Jon Alterman.

per day during the same period (see Figure 3.2). Indeed, the United States no longer receives special treatment as a customer of Saudi petroleum: In 2009 Riyadh decided to abandon the $1-per-barrel discount it had reserved for sales to U.S. oil refineries.[38] But the United States continues to hold very special status for Saudi Arabia as its most important security and economic partner.[39]

Sino-Saudi energy cooperation is growing by leaps and bounds. In the petroleum sector, cooperation is expanding from merely oil exports to such areas as refining. Cooperation is also growing in other energy sectors, including natural gas and even nuclear power. And bilateral trade and investment are also growing.

Figure 3.2
Saudi Petroleum Exports to the United States and China, 1998–2013

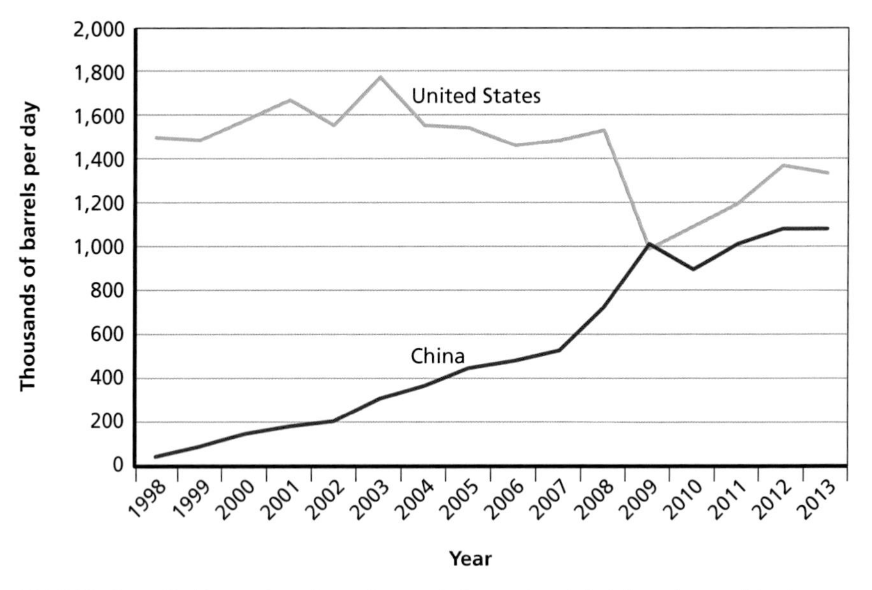

SOURCE: Compiled by authors from Energy Information Administration and Lexis Nexis.
RAND *RR1229-3.2*

---

[38] Manochehr Dorraj and James English, "The Dragon Nests: China's Energy Engagement of the Middle East," *China Report*, Vol. 49, No. 1, February 2013, p. 49.

[39] Personal communication to authors from Jon Alterman.

Refineries

There is growing bilateral cooperation in refining. Saudi Arabia has more "sour" crude oil than it can sell, and China is willing to construct new refineries to process it. During the 1999 visit of PRC President Jiang Zemin, the two governments signed an agreement to permit Saudi companies to invest in Chinese oil refineries in exchange for allowing Chinese companies to explore Saudi energy reserves and pursue other investment projects. As a result, in the early 2000s, Sinopec and Saudi Aramco jointly constructed a refinery near the northern port of Qingdao in Shandong Province. At least one additional refinery was built, this time in Fujian Province in 2008 as a joint venture among ExxonMobil, Aramco, and Sinopec. Two more refineries are scheduled to start construction—one in 2015 in Caofeida, near Tianjin, by Sinopec to process Saudi crude and another, part of a joint venture with Saudi Aramco in Anning in landlocked Yunnan Province, to process Saudi crude oil pumped in via pipeline from Myanmar, which is scheduled to break ground in 2016. In 2006, Riyadh and Beijing signed an agreement to jointly build a petroleum storage complex on Hainan Island, adjacent to land where Sinopec was constructing an oil refinery.[40]

Petrochemicals and Natural Gas

Bilateral cooperation in petrochemical and natural gas projects are also proceeding apace. China has a voracious appetite not just for oil but also for petrochemicals, including those used for fertilizers. Saudi Arabia exports tens of billions of U.S. dollars in such chemicals to China annually.[41] At least three petrochemical facilities have been built or expanded so far: a joint venture between Sinopec and Saudi Aramco in the eastern port of Quanzhou in Fujian Province;[42] a collaborative effort among ExxonMobil, Aramco, and Sinopec, built in Fujian Prov-

---

[40] The information in this paragraph comes from the following sources: Calabrese, 2005; Kemp, 2010, pp. 81–84; U.S. Energy Information Administration, "Country Analysis Brief: China," Washington, D.C., February 4, 2014; Alterman and Garver, 2008, p. 33.

[41] Seznec, 2011, p. 59.

[42] The information in this paragraph comes from Calabrese, 2005.

ince in 2008;[43] and two more funded by Saudi Basic Industries Corporation (SABIC) in Tianjin and Chongqing, two of China's largest cities, in 2012.[44] Moreover, Chinese companies are pursuing natural gas projects. For example, in 2004, Sinopec successfully bid for a contract to tap Saudi Arabia's Rub al-Khali fields.[45]

Nuclear

Bilateral energy cooperation is not just limited to the Saudi provision of oil to China, and not even to collaboration in the petroleum sector. The spectrum of cooperation is considerably wider and includes nuclear energy. This development is noteworthy for two reasons: It raises concerns about nuclear safety, and it triggers alarm about the potential for nuclear proliferation. The two countries signed an accord "to enhance cooperation between the two countries in the development and use of atomic energy for peaceful purposes." The deal was signed by PRC Premier Wen Jiabao during a visit to Riyadh on January 15, 2012. The agreement covered such dimensions as the maintenance and development of nuclear power plants and research reactors, as well as the provision of nuclear fuel. The accord follows on the heels of similar Saudi agreements with France, Argentina, and South Korea.[46] The logic driving Saudi interest in nuclear power appears to be twofold. First, it is a point of pride—a technology that befits a major power. Second, despite a current abundance of hydrocarbons, there is a belief in the kingdom that Saudi Arabia may need alternate sources of power at some point in the future. There seems to be limited interest in Riyadh for acquiring nuclear weapons, although the Saudis do appear to be enthusiastic about acquiring a strategic rocket force and, according to some reports, have already acquired one from China.[47]

---

[43] U.S. Energy Information Administration, 2014.

[44] "About SABIC in China," SABIC, January 20, 2012.

[45] Calabrese, 2005.

[46] Summer Said, "Saudi Arabia, China Sign Nuclear Cooperation Pact," *Wall Street Journal*, January 16, 2012.

[47] Colin H. Kahl, Melissa G. Dalton, and Matthew Irvine, *Atomic Kingdom: If Iran Builds the Bomb, Will Saudi Arabia Be Next?* Washington, D.C.: Center for New American Security,

Trade and Investment

Sino-Saudi economic activities have spilled over into nonenergy sectors in the form of robust trade and investment. Since the late 1990s, Saudi Arabia and China have conducted billions of dollars of trade annually, exclusive of petroleum and other energy sectors. Moreover, each country has made major economic investments in the other, also worth billions of dollars. For example, in 2012, SABIC announced that it would invest $100 million to build a new high-technology zone in Shanghai.[48] Previously, in 2006, Aluminum Corporation of China Limited (CHALCO), China's massive state-owned aluminum producer, in cooperation with Saudi companies, constructed a multi-billion-dollar aluminum plant in Saudi Arabia.[49] Other Chinese corporations were active in the construction of petrochemical plants in Saudi Arabia, winning contracts worth hundreds of millions of dollars.[50]

In 2009, China Railway Corporation (CRC) bid successfully for a project to build a mass-transit system in Mecca.[51] The $1.8 billion deal was to construct a local transportation network capable of handling the annual influx of Muslims from around the world for the hajj. Also in 2009, CRC won a contract worth $500 million from the Saudi Ministry of Education to build 200 primary and secondary schools in the kingdom.[52]

Military and Security Cooperation

Sino-Saudi defense ties are difficult to assess. They appear to be strong but limited in scope. One respected analyst has described bilateral

---

February 2013.

[48] "About SABIC in China," 2012.

[49] Jon B. Alterman, "China's Soft Power in the Middle East," in Carolina G. McGiffert, ed., *Chinese Soft Power and Its Implications for the United States: Competition and Cooperation in the Developing World*, Washington, D.C.: Center for Strategic and International Studies, 2009, p. 67.

[50] See, for example, several issues of *China Chemical Reporter*: October 16, 2005, p. 5; December 26, 2007; June 26, 2009, p. 23.

[51] Kemp, 2010, pp. 81–82. See also Davidson, 2010, p. 40.

[52] Davidson, 2010, p. 59.

military ties between China and Saudi Arabia as "murky."[53] However, both sides see the security relationship as mutually beneficial, albeit not exclusive. While Riyadh is interested in increased Chinese involvement in the security of the Middle East, and Beijing appears receptive in principle, thus far defense relations have focused heavily on Chinese arms sales.

During a March 2014 visit to the Chinese capital, Minister of Defense Salman said: "Saudi Arabia is ready to enhance cooperation with China to protect peace, security, and stability in the region." Salman, who became head of state in January 2015, stated that the Saudis wanted China to use its "great political and economic weight to play a prominent role in achieving peace and security in the region." But Riyadh is not seeking an exclusive defense relationship with Beijing; Saudi Arabia has also reached out to India and Indonesia, signing defense cooperation agreements with both countries in 2013.[54] PRC Minister of National Defense Chang Wanquan reportedly told his Saudi counterpart during the 2014 visit that since China so greatly "valued" its "friendship with Saudi Arabia[,] . . . no matter how the international situation changes, China [was] committed [for the] long-term."[55] To date, the bilateral defense relationship appears heavily skewed toward secretive arms sales of sensitive weaponry, with far more limited activity in other realms, such as military-to-military exchanges and exercises. Indeed, the Saudis seem most interested in China as a source of niche armaments.

The PLA's personnel training for the Saudi armed forces appears very modest, or at least it is conducted on an extremely low profile. Moreover, military exchanges between China and Saudi Arabia do not seem to be institutionalized or vigorous, at least at the senior level. An exhaustive review of the period from 2001 to 2008 reveals no visits by senior PLA leaders to Riyadh, including no recorded visits by the defense minister or the chiefs and deputy chiefs of any of the four

---

[53] Calabrese, 2005.

[54] Tiezzi, 2014a.

[55] "Chang Wanquan Meets with Crown Prince of Saudi Arabia," *China Military Online*, March 17, 2014.

major departments: the General Staff Department, the General Political Department, the General Logistics Department, and the General Armaments Department.[56] While China has participated in an array of bilateral and multilateral exercises since 2003, none of these exercises has been conducted with units of the Saudi armed forces.[57] Arms sales are discussed in the next section.

Despite the limited scope of ties, official Chinese rhetoric has been effusive on the topic of military-to-military relations. The official Chinese press release for the Saudi defense minister's visit to Beijing in 2014 stated: "In recent years the two militaries have witnessed continuous high-level reciprocal visits and excellent cooperation in the fields of personnel training as well as equipment and technology."[58] Evidence of military training is scant, although there are reports of some 1,000 Chinese military advisers working at Saudi missile installations since the 1990s.[59]

Chinese Arms Sales Since 1990: From Howitzers to Intercontinental Ballistic Missiles?

Saudi Arabia is by far the largest importer of arms in the Persian Gulf.[60] The record of reported weapon transactions between Beijing and Riyadh since 1990 has been almost negligible, especially when compared with weapon sales from the United States to Saudi Arabia (see Figure 3.3). By far the most-important sources of imported Saudi armaments have been

---

[56] Heidi Holz and Kenneth Allen, "Military Exchanges with Chinese Characteristics: The People's Liberation Army Experience with Military Relations," in Roy Kamphausen, David Lai, and Andrew Scobell, eds., *The PLA at Home and Abroad: Assessing the Operational Capabilities of China's Military*, Carlisle Barracks, Pa.: U.S. Army War College Strategic Studies Institute, 2010. The highest-ranking PLA officer to visit Saudi Arabia was a military region commander (p. 479).

[57] China's 2012 defense white paper provides a comprehensive list of China's military exercises in an appendix. Saudi Arabia is notable for its absence. See Information Office of the State Council, 2013.

[58] "Chang Wanquan Meets with Crown Prince of Saudi Arabia," 2014.

[59] Kemp, 2010, p. 84.

[60] Carina Solmirano and Pieter D. Wezeman, "Military Spending and Arms Procurement in the Gulf States," *SIPRI Fact Sheet*, Stockholm: Stockholm International Peace Research Institute, October 2010, p. 2.

Figure 3.3
SIPRI TIVs of Official Arms Exports to Saudi Arabia, 1990–2013

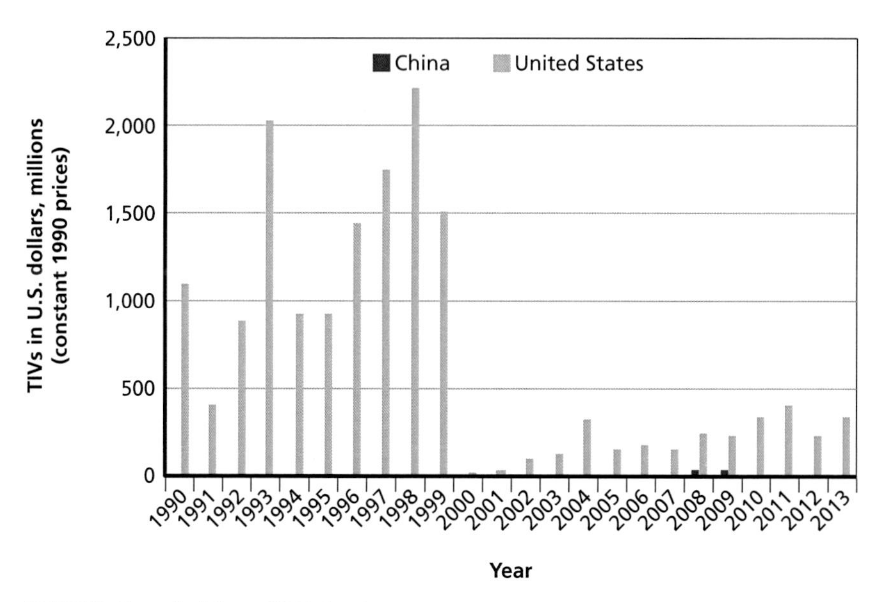

SOURCE: Compiled from SIPRI databases.
RAND *RR1229-3.3*

the United States and the United Kingdom. The United Kingdom, for example, has provided high-performance combat aircraft, while the United States in recent years has sold jet fighters and helicopters. In the period from 2005 to 2009, 43 percent of the volume of Saudi arms imports was from the United Kingdom, 40 percent was from the United States, and only 6 percent of Saudi Arabia's total volume of weapon imports came from China.[61] Between 1990 and 2013, the Stockholm International Peace Research Institute (SIPRI) only recorded China selling 54 PLZ-45 155-mm self-propelled howitzers, which were taken delivery of by Saudi Arabia in 2008 and 2009.[62]

---

[61] Solmirano and Wezeman, 2010, pp. 3–4.

[62] See "China Exports PLZ45 155mm Guns to Saudi Arabia," *Kanwa Asian Defense Review*, August 2008, p. 11.

There are two ways to value the transactions—by financial value and by trend indicator value (TIV). The first refers to the estimated amount actually paid by the customer for the weaponry; the second, according SIPRI, is the estimated production costs of the weaponry, which is intended to "represent the transfer [value] of military resources rather than the financial value of the transfer."[63] Using the former method, the total amount of the 2008–2009 transaction was $400 million; using the latter method, the value is much more modest—only $66 million. In contrast, the United States sold several billions worth of weaponry since 1990. Moreover, this amount was a drop in the big bucket of Saudi military expenditures during these two years. According to SIPRI data, the combined total amount of Riyadh's defense spending in 2008 and 2009 was more than $72 billion.[64]

But China's actual arms sales to Saudi Arabia may be more significant than these data suggest. Reports abound of the secret transfer of Chinese ballistic missiles and Chinese cruise missiles. Knowledgeable proliferation experts, such as Jeffrey Lewis, director of the East Asian Non-Proliferation Project at the Center for Non-Proliferation Studies in Monterey, California, believe that these reports are credible, based on analyses of satellite imagery of missile bases in Saudi Arabia and other open-source circumstantial evidence. Lewis says that he suspects that "Saudi Arabia has invested heavily in conventional ballistic and cruise missiles to provide the kingdom a shot of strategic deterrence." Lewis stresses that he believes that Riyadh is pursuing conventional deterrence and that there is no indication that the Saudis are interested in acquiring a nuclear arsenal.[65] Moreover, it is entirely plausible that China has provided IRBMs to Saudi Arabia. While Beijing appears to have embraced the norm of nonproliferation where nuclear weapons are concerned, no such norm is evident where ballistic and cruise

---

[63] "SIPRI Arms Transfers Database—Methodology," web page, Stockholm International Peace Research Institute, undated.

[64] Solmirano and Wezeman, 2010, p. 2.

[65] Jeffrey Lewis, "Saudi Arabia's Strategic Dyad," *Arms Control Wonk*, July 15, 2013; Jeffrey Lewis, "Why Did Saudi Arabia Buy Chinese Missiles?" *Foreign Policy*, January 30, 2014.

missiles are involved.[66] A retired Saudi major general reportedly stated during a September 2014 press conference that the "Saudi military did indeed receive DF-21 missiles from China[,] . . . including . . . maintenance check and upgraded facilities."[67]

Moreover, there appears to be continued Saudi interest in acquiring military equipment and weapon systems from China. When the Saudi defense minister met with his Chinese counterpart in Beijing in March 2014, General Liu Sheng, the deputy director of the PLA's General Armaments Department, also reportedly attended the meeting.[68] In addition, Russian media reported that China and Saudi Arabia signed a deal in April 2014 to provide an unknown number of unmanned aerial vehicles.[69] There is concern over the secretive nature of these reported sales, as well as over the apparent complete disregard for nonproliferation regimes. But perhaps of greatest concern is that these transactions might threaten the delicate balance of power in the Persian Gulf and wider Middle East. The situation in the region is unsettled, with the specter of ongoing sectarian violence in Syria and Iraq spilling over into neighboring states. Saudi Arabia is viewed with great suspicion by a number of other well-armed states, notably Iran. Either of these states could react to what might be perceived as a Saudi arms buildup in a number of ways that could exacerbate regional tensions.

One U.S. analyst recently remarked that "China-Saudi Arabia defense cooperation may be on the rise."[70] This judgment is based on what seems to be a growing convergence of interests: both Beijing and

---

[66] See, for example, Evan Medeiros, *Reluctant Restraint: The Evolution of China's Nonproliferation Policies and Practices, 1980–2004*, Stanford, Calif.: Stanford University Press, 2007.

[67] "Saudi Arabia Admits to Purchase of Chinese DF-21 Missile," *Want China Times*, September 22, 2014. For analysis, see Ethan Meick, *China's Reported Ballistic Missile Sale to Saudi Arabia: Background and Potential Implications*, Washington, D.C.: U.S.-China Economic and Security Review Commission, June 16, 2014.

[68] "Chang Wanquan Meets with Crown Prince of Saudi Arabia," 2014.

[69] "Saudi Arabia Signs Deal for China's Pterodactyl Drone," *Want China Times*, May 7, 2014.

[70] Meick, 2014, p. 4.

Riyadh are worried about what seems to be an increasingly volatile regional security environment and a common commitment to expanding bilateral energy cooperation, combined with qualms about the future of U.S. security undertakings in the Middle East and Persian Gulf. And yet Chinese defense relations are heavily skewed toward arms sales. The motives behind these transactions are monetary and geostrategic influence.

Conclusion

An examination of China's use of diplomatic, economic, and military instruments of national power in its relationship with Saudi Arabia reveals a largely positive picture for Beijing. Beijing has adeptly promoted the interests outlined in Chapter Two and is attaining its objectives. Specifically, China has

- secured access to energy resources in, and expanded economic ties with, Saudi Arabia
- partnered geostrategically with Saudi Arabia to balance against U.S. influence
- suppressed most criticism of Beijing's treatment of its Muslims, including Uighurs
- received regular affirmation from Saudi Arabia that China is a rising great power.

In short, a review of China's effort towards Saudi Arabia indicates that Beijing's Middle East strategy to date has been largely a success for China. Nevertheless, questions arise about whether this strategy is sustainable.

While bilateral energy and economic ties are solid and deepening, China's diplomatic and military links with Saudi Arabia are shallow and relatively modest, respectively. Geostrategically, China is soft balancing against the United States. Beijing and Riyadh concur more about what they are against than what they are for. Thus, the two governments are united in their "opposition . . . to global political norms" promoted by the United States and other Western democracies.[71] Both the CCP and Saudi Royal Family see U.S. advocacy of human rights and democratization as dangerous and feel threatened by the Arab Spring. However, there are many issues where China and Saudi Arabia differ—on Syria and Iran, for example. Moreover, despite formal Saudi proclamations of "traditional friendship and strategic convergence" between Riyadh and Beijing, there is a discernible feeling that China is "neither a friend nor foe" of Saudi Arabia.[72] Beijing-Riyadh cooperation is founded on mutual insecurities and born of pragmatic necessity. While such a state of affairs can support ongoing economic collaboration, it is not necessarily going to provide the bricks and mortar of a solid and enduring strategic partnership.

The touchstone of the bilateral relationship is energy cooperation—an arena where the interests of Beijing and Riyadh are complementary: The PRC desires stable, reliable, and long-term access to energy reserves, and Saudi Arabia is eager to secure an enduring and dependable energy partner. Moreover, the two regimes are generally comfortable with each other's political systems and geostrategic outlooks—neither side seeks to transform the other, nor does either side view the other as threatening its domestic stability or territorial integrity. Sino-Saudi security interests also overlap. Diplomatically relations are relatively stable, although visits by Chinese senior leaders to Saudi Arabia are currently on hold. But the weakest instrument employed as part of China's strategy toward the Middle East and Saudi Arabia remains China's extremely limited military power in the region.

Nevertheless, both countries see mutual benefit in continued limited but noteworthy security cooperation. While Saudi Arabia seems positive on strengthening defense ties with China, a qualitative ramping up seems an unlikely prospect without a major downturn in the U.S. security commitment to Saudi Arabia and the GCC. Moreover, China's defense establishment simply cannot provide the same kind of high-tech weaponry and the level of interoperability or match the combat and operational experience offered by the United States. And

---

[71] Alterman and Garver, 2008, pp. 35–36.

[72] Al-Sudairi, 2013, p. 31.

the wary-dragon strategy means that Beijing will be hesitant to qualitatively upgrade security relations. But China is willing to remain a valued supplier of key niche weapon systems—ones that the United States may be unwilling to provide. These systems include IRBMs and unmanned aerial vehicles, which Beijing has already reportedly provided to Riyadh.

CHAPTER FOUR

China and Iran—Close but Complicated

China and Iran have close but complicated relations. The two countries are alike in many ways. They are both ancient civilizations and historic empires. Iranian and Chinese officials consistently emphasize the importance of their political and cultural ties, stressing the commonality of their ancient heritage and cooperation on contemporary issues. Like the Chinese, the Iranians pride themselves as one of the "first" ancient civilizations. Iran views itself as a "natural" power in the Middle East. Iran's sense of power is shaped not only by its historic role but also by its size, large population, and its revolutionary mission of ridding the region of Western and, in particular, American "imperialism." Both Iran and China deeply resent their respective subjugation by Western powers in the 19th and 20th centuries.

Communist China's anti-Western origins and its lack of past imperial involvement in Iran make it an attractive partner for the Iranian regime.[1] And China's current struggle to roll back American power in East Asia may be particularly appealing for the Iranian leadership, especially as Tehran faces a continued rivalry with the United States, even after achieving a nuclear agreement. Iranian officials, especially the conservative establishment, like to think of China as a strategic partner that can help lessen Iran's isolation, help its economy grow, and provide it with modern weapons and technology to make Iran a predominant regional power. After all, the two countries have a long history of economic, military, and even nuclear cooperation.

[1] Scott Warren Harold and Alireza Nader, *China and Iran: Economic, Political, and Military Relations*, Santa Monica, Calif.: RAND Corporation, OP-351-CMEPP, 2012.

But not all is well with Chinese-Iranian relations. China, a member of the United Nations Security Council's P5+1 group (the five permanent members—United States, the United Kingdom, France, Russia, and China—plus Germany) negotiating with Iran on the nuclear program, has supported U.S.-led efforts to isolate Iran economically and increase pressure on Tehran to make nuclear concessions. The Chinese government, along with much of Chinese industry, has complied with U.S. and United Nations sanctions against Iran's nuclear program. While still remaining Iran's biggest oil purchaser, China has nevertheless sharply decreased its purchase of Iranian oil in order to not violate U.S. sanctions. Moreover, China has frozen much of its business activities in Iran and failed to deliver on several large projects.

To make matters worse for Iran, Chinese companies do not pay cash for Iranian oil, because of financial sanctions, which have shut Iran out of the global financial system. Instead, Iran has been forced into a barter system in which it must use its oil proceeds from China to buy Chinese goods, ranging from consumer products to automobiles.[2] Many Iranians, unable to access Western goods, complain about "inferior" Chinese products that tend to break down easily or do not meet Iranian tastes. Iranians have been blaming the flood of Chinese imports for suppressing domestic production and exacerbating unemployment since the Ahmadinejad presidency (2005–2013) led to Iran's growing isolation.[3] In an August 2010 statement, the Ministry of Commerce announced that import licenses for 170 goods had been revoked because they failed to meet Iran's quality standards.[4] More than 80 percent of the banned goods were Chinese, consisting mostly of toys, electronics, and household items. The Sino-Iranian Chamber of Commerce has attempted to dismiss these complaints as "Western

---

[2] "China Floods Iran with Cheap Consumer Goods in Exchange for Oil," *Guardian*, February 20, 2013.

[3] "Enteghad az Dowlat beh Dalile 'Vagozaariye Bazaare Iran beh Chiin'" ["Criticism of Administration for 'Handing Iranian Market Over to China'"], *Deutsche Welle*, June 6, 2012.

[4] "Fehreste 170 Kalaaye Varedaatiye Bi-Keyfiyat" ["List of 170 Poor Quality Imported Goods"], *Tabnak*, August 24, 2010.

propaganda," intending to damage relations between the two countries.[5] And negative perceptions of China are not restricted to the average person; there also appears to be a growing resentment of China among some of the political elite and clerics.[6] Reformist and centrist political figures view the Chinese government as abetting the worst economic and political abuses of Mahmoud Ahmadinejad's presidency.

In particular, the reform movement sees China as having helped the Iranian government crush the 2009 Green Movement uprising, through supplying Iran with anti-riot gear and surveillance technology.[7] During the upheaval, some protesters even chanted "death to China."[8] Moreover, many Iranians and more-centrist or reformist political leaders see Iran as having become overly dependent on a China that is eager to exploit Iran's economic isolation. Robust enforcement of the sanctions regime against Tehran has virtually eliminated Western trade and investment in the country, leaving Beijing few competitors and highly favorable conditions in which to negotiate business with Iran.[9]

Chinese policy toward Iran continues to be a cautious balance—broadly respecting U.S.-led sanctions and restrictions while capitalizing on the opportunities presented by Iran's isolation. Beijing did not wish to see a nuclear-armed Iran or open confrontation and military crisis, but nor was it as concerned as Washington with proliferation or Iran's regional ambitions. The Chinese national-security establishment broadly views Iran as a stable country in a turbulent region, which can help protect China's economic and geostrategic interests.[10] In particular, China's national security establishment appears to view Iran as an effective counterweight against groups such as the Islamic State.[11] But

---

[5] "Bi Keyfiat Budan e Kola haye Chini Tabligh e Gharb Ast" ["The Poor Quality of Chinese Goods Is Western Propaganda"], Digarban.com, March 11, 2012.

[6] "Enteghad Az Dowlat Beh Dalile 'Vagozaariye Bazaare Iran Beh Chiin,'" 2012.

[7] Harold and Nader, 2012.

[8] Harold and Nader, 2012.

[9] Dorraj and English, 2013.

[10] Discussions with Chinese analysts, Beijing and Shanghai, September 8–17, 2014.

[11] Discussions with Chinese analysts, Beijing, September 8–15, 2014.

although China could in some ways benefit from the nuclear agreement and the loosening of sanctions, the maintenance of a stable, low-level, simmering crisis is also tolerable, perpetuating Beijing's strong market access amid Iran's economic decline.

President Hassan Rouhani's government has approached China cordially and has shown an enthusiasm for warmer Chinese-Iranian relations. Despite China's compliance with sanctions, Rouhani's government views better ties with China as an important component of decreasing Iran's isolation. China can become an even more important energy and economic partner in the wake of the nuclear agreement between Iran and the P5+1; Chinese investment in Iran's energy sector could be an important part of Rouhani's effort to privatize the economy and integrate it more closely into the global system. China will also continue to serve as a useful counterweight to U.S. influence in the Middle East and beyond. At the same time, Rouhani may want to rebalance Chinese-Iranian ties to lessen Iran's dependence on Beijing by developing better relations with the West. Iranians are in general sensitive to being dominated by foreign powers, Western or not.

From China's perspective, Iran can help counter U.S. power in the Middle East as China chips at U.S. influence in East Asia.[12] Iran is the only major regional power that is not aligned with the United States. If China decides to increase its military presence in the Middle East, then Iran could play an invaluable role in achieving Beijing's geostrategic goals.

But it would be a stretch to call China and Iran equal partners. China views Iran as a junior partner, at most. China's economic ties to the United States far outweigh Iran's importance to China.[13] And Beijing is careful not to upset Iran's major regional rivals, Israel and Saudi Arabia. In discussions with the authors in 2014, Chinese analysts emphasized that Riyadh was Beijing's *strategic partner*, but they did not

---

[12] John Garver, "China-Iran Relations: Cautious Friendship with America's Nemesis," *China Report*, Vol. 49, No. 1, February 2013.

[13] Manochehr Dorraj and James English, "China's Strategy for Energy Acquisition in the Middle East: Potential for Conflict and Cooperation with the United States," *Asian Politics & Policy*, Vol. 4, No. 2, April 2012.

use the same term to describe China's relations with Iran.[14] For now China is content with the nature of its relationship with Iran.

The Growth of Ties in the Wake of Iran's Revolution

China and Iran established cordial if not particularly warm ties before the 1979 Iranian Revolution. Iran's last monarch, Mohammad Reza Pahlavi, saw China as an important international player but was mostly focused on the Cold War rivalry between the United States and Soviet Union. An avowed anti-communist, the shah saw his alliance with the West, particularly the United States, as a pillar of his rule and of Iran's ability to project power in the Middle East. The 1979 revolution produced a fundamental shift in Chinese-Iranian relations. The shah's replacement by a revolutionary and anti-American Shi'a theocracy removed Iran from the Western camp; Tehran's foreign policy became focused on "liberating" the Middle East from America. But Tehran was also wary of Moscow and its communist surrogates in Iran and throughout the region. China was an independent, revolutionary, and developing power competing with both Washington and Moscow and therefore a more attractive partner for Iran.

Ties between communist China and the Islamic republic were rocky at first. Chinese Communist Party Chairman Hua Guofeng was one of the last foreign dignitaries to meet with the shah before he fled Iran. Ayatollah Ruhollah Khomeini, the leader of the revolution and founder of the Islamic republic, initially viewed China as an unfriendly power. However, Iran's postrevolutionary isolation and a sense of affinity with China led to growing ties between the two nations.

Iran's war with Iraq (1980–1988) was one of the major factors driving Chinese-Iranian cooperation. Iran had been a major recipient of U.S. arms before the revolution and had a difficult time replenishing its forces during the long and bloody war. Tehran was largely dependent on minor players, such as Syria, Libya, and North Korea, while Iraq received arms from the United States, France, the Soviet Union,

[14] Discussions with Chinese analysts, Beijing, September 8–15, 2014.

and a host of other powers. China was the only major power willing to sell weapons to Iran (although Beijing sold arms and military aircraft to Iraq at the same time).[15] Furthermore, China abandoned its support of revolutionary communism in the 1980s and posed even less of a threat to Iran's new model of Islamic rule.

Iran's efforts to recover from the war meant that it could not base its foreign policy on ideology alone. Tehran needed access to foreign investment, trade, and technology for postwar reconstruction. Iranian pragmatists, such as President Ali Akbar Hashemi Rafsanjani, sought closer ties with foreign powers, particularly of non-Western nations. Rafsanjani was particularly keen on privatizing the economy without undertaking political reforms. And, unlike the West, China did not preach to Iran about democracy or human rights.

Rafsanjani's 1992 visit to China marked a milestone in Chinese-Iranian relations. Subsequently, China became an important commercial and military partner for Iran. In particular, China provided Iran not only with weapons but also with the know-how and technology to develop its military and nuclear program.[16] Iran's strategy was shaped by the need to break its isolation. And while China was beginning to assert itself on the world stage, its growing economic and military cooperation with Iran was based on practical calculations, not some sort of grand strategy toward the Middle East.

China's economy grew steadily in the 1990s. China needed Iranian oil and saw the reconstructing Middle East nation as a good business opportunity. In 1993, China became a net oil importer, increasing Iran's importance in Chinese calculations.[17] U.S.-China tensions over the Tiananmen massacre also served as an impetus for greater Chinese-Iranian cooperation.

However, China's ties with Iran have waxed and waned based on circumstances. China would deal with Iran when it was suitable for its interests but was willing to curtail ties with Iran if pressured by

---

[15] See the SIPRI Arms Transfers Database at www.sipri.org/databases/armstransfers (accessed September 16, 2014).

[16] Harold and Nader, 2012.

[17] Harold and Nader, 2012.

Washington. The 1980s and 1990s saw a growing partnership between China and Iran, but relations had begun to cool somewhat in the late 1990s. It appeared that Beijing had made a decision to restrain bilateral relations; Chinese support for Iran's nuclear and missile program began to wane in 1997, as part of an effort by Beijing to improve relations with Washington.[18]

The Chinese leadership, faced with increasing tension with the United States over Taiwan and eager to join the World Trade Organization (WTO), may have decided that a less active relationship with Tehran would enhance Chinese ties with the United States and benefit Beijing's much larger economic and geopolitical goals.

Nevertheless, China's relations with Iran again witnessed a significant improvement in the first decade of the 21st century. As China's energy needs began to grow dramatically, its leadership emphasized a "going out" policy of investing in energy-rich markets. Iran's vast energy reserves, relative geographic proximity to China, and hostility toward the United States made it an attractive business partner.

Military and Nuclear Cooperation

China was a key partner in Iran's military modernization and nuclear development over the past three decades, supplying Iran with small arms and anti-ship cruise missiles, as well as supporting the development of Iran's own domestic military production capabilities.[19] China was also instrumental in launching Iran's nuclear program in the 1980s and 1990s.[20] The provision of advanced weapons to Iran (and their occasional migration to substate actors[21]) supports the Chinese defense industry and bolsters Iran as a useful regional counterweight to the United States.

---

[18] Garver, 2013.

[19] Harold and Nader, 2012.

[20] Harold and Nader, 2012.

[21] Robert F. Worth and C. J. Chivers, "Seized Chinese Weapons Raise Concerns on Iran," *New York Times*, March 2, 2013.

In 2008, China surpassed Russia as Iran's biggest arms supplier.[22] From 2002 to 2009, the majority of Chinese arms sales to Iran were anti-ship and anti-aircraft missiles.[23] These included C-801, C-802, and C-704 anti-ship cruise missiles and QW-11 man-portable surface-to-air missiles.[24] In March 2010, Iran opened a Chinese-built plant for Nasr-1 radar-guided anti-ship missiles.[25] The Nasr-1 is based on the Chinese C-704.[26] China also helped Iran create its Noor anti-ship cruise missile, which is an upgraded version of the Chinese C-802.[27]

Since 2005, Iran has also gained assistance on its missile program through membership in the Asia Pacific Space Cooperation Organization (APSCO).[28] It is through this organization that China assisted Iran in developing ballistic missiles that could launch satellites.[29]

From 1984 to 1996, China provided Iran with critical assistance in developing its nuclear program.[30] China helped Iran build the Esfahan Nuclear Research Center, which opened in 1984. China trained Iranian nuclear engineers and helped Iran mine uranium. Iran and China signed a nuclear cooperation agreement in 1990. One year later, China shipped one metric ton of uranium hexafluoride (UF6) to Iran.[31] Between 1998 and 2002, Iran used the Chinese-supplied UF6 in its testing of centrifuges at the Kalaye Electric Company in Tehran.[32] In

---

[22] Worth and Chivers, 2013.

[23] Worth and Chivers, 2013.

[24] Worth and Chivers, 2013; Garver, 2013.

[25] "China Opens Missile Plant in Iran," *UPI*, April 23, 2010.

[26] "Iran > Procurement," *Jane's Sentinel Security Assessment—The Gulf States*, IHS Jane's, September 10, 2014.

[27] "China Opens Missile Plant in Iran," 2010.

[28] Garver, 2013.

[29] Garver, 2013.

[30] Harold and Nader, 2012.

[31] David Albright and Andrea Stricker, "Iran's Nuclear Program," in United States Institute of Peace, *The Iran Primer*, Washington, D.C., updated September 2015.

[32] International Atomic Energy Agency, *Implementation of the NPT Safeguards Agreement in the Islamic Republic of Iran*, Vienna, November 10, 2003.

1997, Beijing ended official support for Iran's nuclear program in an effort to improve ties with Washington.

Though China has tempered its military cooperation with Iran in recent years, following the intensification of sanctions, both countries continue to emphasize the strength of their relationship. Iranian Defense Minister Hossein Dehghan visited Beijing in May 2014; he was welcomed by his Chinese counterpart, Chang Wanquan. Dehghan reflected on the global security situation and called for the renewal of the ancient bond symbolized in the Silk Road. He also asked for Iran and China to increase their cooperation in defense, security, and military matters.[33]

Iranian media further claimed that Chang had described Iran as a "strategic partner."[34] This certainly reflected Iran's desires for the relationship,[35] but China has tended to be more circumspect in characterizing its security cooperation with Iran and, in recent years, appears to be less eager to use the term *strategic partner*.[36] Nevertheless, for the first time, Chinese warships visited Iranian ports to conduct naval exercises, in September 2014,[37] buttressing Iranian views of a budding strategic relationship between the two nations.

Despite the Chinese government's curtailment of military assistance to Iran, Chinese front businesses remain important in Iran's proliferation and defense modernization programs. It is unclear whether the Chinese government is aware of these activities or has decided to turn a blind eye to them. In April 2014, the U.S. Treasury sanctioned eight China-based companies for acting as fronts for Karl Lee (Li

33 "Takid e Vaziraee e Defa' e Iran va Chin bar Gostaresh e Hamkari haye Defa'ee Tehran va Pekan" ["Tehran and Beijing—Iranian and Chinese Defense Secretaries Emphasize Increase in Defense Cooperation"], Fars News Agency, May 5, 2014.

34 "Takid e Vaziraee e Defa' e Iran va Chin bar Gostaresh e Hamkari haye Defa'ee Tehran va Pekan," 2014.

35 "Iran Views China Ties as Strategic: Official," PressTV, April 8, 2014.

36 "Xi Jinping Holds Talks with President Hassan Rouhani of Iran, Stressing to Promote China-Iran Friendly Cooperation to New High," Ministry of Foreign Affairs of the People's Republic of China, May 22, 2014.

37 Thomas Erdbrink and Chris Buckley, "China and Iran to Conduct Joint Naval Exercises in the Persian Gulf," *New York Times*, September 21, 2014.

Feng Wei) in support of Iran's missile proliferation activities.[38] Lee was accused of violating the International Emergency Economic Powers Act and attempting to supply dual-use technology to Iran's defense and aerospace industries.[39] While "known proliferator" and "principal supplier" Lee was not acting in an official government capacity, Beijing was quick to come to his defense, saying that it "resolutely opposes" unilateral sanctions and warning that the U.S. actions would harm nonproliferation efforts.[40]

According to Vann Van Diepen, principal deputy assistant secretary of state for international security and nonproliferation, Lee was "one of the top serial proliferators, a major source of supply for the Iranian missile program. Unfortunately he seems to continue to be able to obtain technologies for Iran by operating in and through Chinese territory."[41] The United States has repeatedly expressed frustration at China's failure to fully adhere to international nonproliferation regimes, though it has admitted that China has shown some progress and cooperation in this area.

In April 2014, the United States also accused the Chinese national Sihai Cheng of violating U.S. sanctions by helping Iran procure thousands of U.S.-made pressure transducers, which are used in uranium enrichment.[42]

---

[38] "US Targets Weapons, Oil Sanctions Evaders," in *The Iran Primer*, Washington, D.C.: United States Institute of Peace, April 29, 2014.

[39] U.S. Department of Justice, "'Karl Lee' Charged in Manhattan Federal Court with Using a Web of Front Companies to Evade U.S. Sanctions," Office of Public Affairs, April 29, 2014.

[40] "China 'Resolutely Opposes' U.S. Sanctions on Missile Parts Supplier," Reuters, April 30, 2014.

[41] William MacLean, "Iran Seeks Banned Nuclear Items, Uses China Trader for Missile Parts: U.S.," Reuters, March 17, 2014.

[42] "U.S. Accuses Chinese Man Of Breaching Iran Nuclear Sanctions," BBC, April 4, 2014.

Economic and Energy Cooperation

China's high energy needs play the most important role in its relations with Iran. China's continued economic development makes access to Persian Gulf oil increasingly important.[43] In 2011, China became the world's largest importer of oil from the Persian Gulf (composing 26 percent of its overall consumption).[44] As of 2014, Iran was contributing 10 percent of China's oil imports.[45] Beijing's ties with Tehran began to become closer following China's acceptance as a member of the WTO in 2001.[46] Chinese imports of Iranian oil doubled from 2000 to 2009 (although Chinese imports from Saudi Arabia increased by seven times in same period).[47] Meanwhile, Chinese businesses began to take advantage of the windfall resulting from international companies pulling out of the Iranian market following pressure from the United States.[48] In 2005, China surpassed Japan as Iran's main source of imports.[49] And, in 2007, China overtook the European Union as Iran's largest trading partner.[50]

Petroleum and Gas

Iran realizes that a chief benefit of doing business with Chinese firms is their greater willingness to transfer technology relative to Western companies. According to John Garver, while not as advanced as West-

---

[43] Samir Tata, "Recalibrating American Grand Strategy: Softening US Policies Toward Iran in Order to Contain China," *Parameters*, Vol. 42, No. 4, 2013.

[44] Tata, 2013.

[45] Xiangming Chen and Ivan Su, "A Different Global Power? Understanding China's Role in the Developing World," *The European Financial Review*, June 2014.

[46] Harold and Nader, 2012.

[47] Garver, 2013.

[48] Harold and Nader, 2012.

[49] Garver, 2013.

[50] Lauren Dickey and Helia Ighani, "Iran Looks East, China Pivots West," *The Diplomat*, August 25, 2014.

ern technology, "Chinese industrial technology is often 'good enough'" and still can be seen as "a significant leap forward for Iran's industry."[51]

In addition to technology, Iran sees China as a source of much-needed investments. Since 2004, China has been a significant investor in Iran's energy infrastructure.[52] Iran needs more than $100 billion in investment to bring its energy infrastructure up to date.[53] In 2004, the Chinese firm Sinopec signed a $100 billion deal with the National Iranian Oil Company to develop the Yadavaran oil field.[54] In 2006, the China National Petroleum Corporation (CNPC) replaced the Japanese oil and gas exploration company INPEX after the United States succeeded in pressuring it to cut its share in Iran's Azadegan oil field by 90 percent.[55] By 2009, China was Iran's main partner in developing its energy sector, investing $30 billion that year alone.[56]

Following U.S. sanctions on gasoline exports to Iran in 2009, Chinese companies signed up for $3 billion in deals to improve Iran's gasoline refinement.[57] And the same year, CNPC signed a $4.7 billion deal to develop Iran's South Pars Phase 11 gas field.[58] In 2011, China signed a deal to invest $2.5 billion in developing the South Azadegan oil field.[59] And, in 2013, Sinopec and a South Korean company signed a $1.5 billion deal to improve the Isfahan Oil Refinery.[60]

---

[51] Garver, 2013, p. 77.

[52] Dickey and Ighani, 2014.

[53] Dorraj and English, 2013.

[54] Janet Xuanli Liao, "China's Energy Diplomacy and Its 'Peaceful Rise' Ambition: The Cases of Sudan and Iran," *Asian Journal of Peacebuilding*, Vol. 1, No. 2, 2013.

[55] Liao, 2013.

[56] Garver, 2013.

[57] Liao, 2013.

[58] Liao, 2013.

[59] Liao, 2013.

[60] Liao, 2013.

Petrochemicals

China is Iran's largest market for petrochemicals, especially methanol.[61] After sanctions on Iran's petrochemical industry were eased as part of an interim nuclear deal signed between Iran and the P5+1 in November 2013, China increased its investment in that segment of the Iranian market. In June 2014, Iran announced that China would finance the completion of seven methanol plants in South Pars.[62] China also planned to invest $2.6 billion in a petrochemical complex in Bushehr.[63] In May 2014, Chinese companies announced plans to invest more than $600 million to construct the Lordegan Petrochemical Complex.[64]

China is also helping Iran develop its nonenergy infrastructure. As of 2010, China was financing $1 billion in Tehran city-improvement projects.[65] And since the mid-2000s, Chinese companies have signed billions of dollars in deals to build dams throughout Iran.[66] These projects provide jobs for hundreds of Chinese laborers.[67]

China and Sanctions

With a few exceptions, China has broadly complied with United Nations and U.S. sanctions against Iran. Beijing voted for the last round of United Nations Security Council resolutions (1929) against Iran, paving the way for stronger U.S. and European sanctions. And despite its public opposition to sanctions as a policy, China has supported the P5+1 strategy of increasing pressure against Iran.

---

[61] Harold and Nader, 2012.

[62] "China to Finance 7 Iranian Methanol Projects," Fars News Agency, June 14, 2014.

[63] "China to Finance 7 Iranian Methanol Projects," 2014.

[64] "China to Finance 7 Iranian Methanol Projects," 2014.

[65] Harold and Nader, 2012.

[66] "Iran, China to Sign $2b Deal on Dams," *Press TV*, May 10, 2007; Harold and Nader, 2012.

[67] Harold and Nader, 2012.

China has arguably been the biggest beneficiary of Iran's nuclear dispute with the West. Manochehr Dorraj and James English argue that "Beijing has masterfully used its relationship with Tehran as a bargaining chip in its relationship with the United States," extracting concessions from Washington in exchange for agreeing to United Nations sanctions.[68] These concessions have allowed China to remain Iran's largest trade partner. China benefits from waivers to import Iranian oil, which is discounted because of Iran's limited export opportunities. According to Kenneth Katzman, "Iran is essentially on a junk-for-oil program."[69] By the third quarter of 2013, China owed around $22 billion to Iran in missed payments as a result of U.S. sanctions on Iran's banking system.[70]

Moreover, China, while preserving its deals with Iran, nevertheless has gone "slow" to appease the United States.[71] China's strategy is "to hold onto the projects for which they have signed binding agreements but to delay making any substantial investments in these projects until it is safe to do so."[72] As part of this strategy, Chinese companies often sign big deals with Iran but drag their feet on transferring the funds to start them.[73]

Despite having signed a $4.7 billion deal to develop the South Pars Phase 11 gas field, China's cumulative investment had only totaled $18 million by August 2011.[74] The $18 million investment was $2 million less than the limit placed on investment in Iran's oil and gas industry by the U.S. Comprehensive Iran Sanctions, Accountability, and

---

68 Dorraj and English, 2012.

69 Indira A. R. Lakshmanan, and Pratish Narayanan, "India and China Skirt Iran Sanctions with 'Junk for Oil,'" Bloomberg, March 30, 2012.

70 Yun Sun, "Iran and Asia 1: China Is the Quiet Giant," in *The Iran Primer*, Washington, D.C.: United States Institute of Peace, January 29, 2014.

71 Garver, 2013.

72 Erica Downs, "Cooperating with China on Iran," The German Marshall Fund of the United States, January 2012, p. 5.

73 Zhao Hong, "China's Dilemma on Iran: Between Energy Security and a Responsible Rising Power," *Journal of Contemporary China*, Vol. 23, No. 87, 2014.

74 Downs, 2012.

Divestment Act legislation (in 2013, CNPC pulled out of the deal completely).[75] By January 2012, Iran had temporarily suspended China National Offshore Oil Corporation from developing the North Pars field because of delays.[76] In April 2014, Iran canceled a $2.5 billion Azadegan oil field deal with China because of delays.[77]

Some Chinese firms have opted to pull out of projects completely to avoid U.S. sanctions. In 2012, the Industrial and Commercial Bank of China buckled to U.S. pressure and pulled out of a deal to help finance the Iran-Pakistan gas pipeline.[78] In April 2013, China's second-largest telecoms equipment maker, ZTE Corporation, "essentially stopped doing business in Iran," according to the company's chairman.[79] The group had been accused by the United States of selling the Iranian government a potent surveillance system, though the company complained that other competitors were selling more of the same equipment.[80] A few months later, two major Chinese shipping firms, China Shipping Container Lines and China Ocean Shipping Group Company Container Lines, also cut links with Iran in response to heightened U.S. sanctions,[81] joining a number of other major international shipping lines that had pulled out the year before. Bilateral trade has declined significantly because of sanctions, dropping from $45 billion in 2011 to $37 billion in 2012.[82] Disputes between Iranian and Chinese firms over the terms of contracts also had a nega-

---

[75] Liao, 2013.

[76] Downs, 2012.

[77] Dickey and Ighani, 2014.

[78] Paul Richter and Alex Rodriguez, "Chinese Bank Pulls Out of Pakistan-Iran Pipeline Project," *Los Angeles Times*, March 14, 2012.

[79] Jason Subler, "China's ZTE Says It Basically Dropped Iran Business," Reuters, April 18, 2013.

[80] Subler, 2013.

[81] Jonathan Saul, "Chinese Firms Drop Iran as Latest U.S. Sanctions Bite," Reuters, July 1, 2013.

[82] Liao, 2013.

tive impact on trade relations.[83] Chinese nonenergy investment also dropped by 87 percent, from $3 billion in 2011 to $400 million in 2012.[84] By 2013, Iran had dropped from third to sixth place as China's oil supplier.[85]

However, China's compliance with sanctions has not been airtight. In January 2014, the United States announced that it would not enforce sanctions regarding Chinese imports of crude oil, as long as China maintained its current import levels.[86] However, China imported a record amount of Iranian oil in the first half of 2014, an increase of 48 percent over the previous year.[87] In June 2014, Sinopec doubled production at Yadavaran oil field, to 50,000 barrels per day.[88] As of 2014, Iran had returned to its third-place position (in oil exports to China) and was contributing 10 percent of China's oil imports.[89]

In 2009, China helped Iran circumvent gasoline sanctions by providing around 40,000 barrels per day of gasoline to Iran.[90] In 2012, the U.S. State Department sanctioned the Chinese company Zhuhai Zhenrong for delivering gasoline to Iran.[91]

Relations Under Rouhani

President Rouhani's government is seeking better ties with the rest of the world, especially foreign powers in Europe and Asia. While it may

---

83 U.S. Energy Information Administration, "Country Analysis Brief: Iran," Washington, D.C., July 21, 2014, p. 17.

84 Liao, 2013.

85 Liao, 2013.

86 Wayne Ma, "China Imports Record Amount of Iranian Crude," *Wall Street Journal*, July 21, 2014.

87 Dickey and Ighani, 2014; Ma, 2014.

88 Dickey and Ighani, 2014.

89 Chen and Su, 2014.

90 Liao, 2013.

91 Downs, 2012.

recognize Iran's overdependence on China, the Rouhani government nevertheless realizes the importance of China in attaining its economic, geopolitical, and even military goals.

Rouhani belongs to a centrist and pragmatic trend in Iranian politics that disavows ideology as a basis for foreign and economic policy. Rouhani and his supporters are dedicated to the preservation of the Islamic Republic and the expansion of Iranian influence in the Middle East. But they have major policy differences with "principlists," such as Ahmadinejad, who view the world through an ideological prism. For Rouhani, the Islamic Republic's survival depends on unity at home, smart use of diplomacy, international recognition, economic vitality, and military strength.

Rouhani's more balanced approach toward foreign policy does not equate to abandoning one power or set of powers for another. Iranian pragmatists may be at times critical of China, but they also appreciate a strong relationship with China. And Rouhani's view of the world is closely aligned with that of Rafsanjani, one of the men responsible for establishing close Chinese-Iranian ties in the 1980s and 1990s. Much like his predecessor and patron, Rouhani appears to believe in economic reform without major political changes. China, a successful "developing country" that has managed to maintain its authoritarian political system in addition to its ideological roots, presents itself as a model worthy of possible emulation.

Immediately following his election, Rouhani declared the development of all aspects of Iran's relations with China to be a special priority in Iran's foreign policy,[92] a theme emphasized by Parliament Speaker Ali Larijani during his October 2013 visit to Beijing at the invitation of Chinese leadership.[93]

The Rouhani government is particularly eager to expand energy and economic ties with China. Most Western and Asian businesses

---

[92] "Tose'e Ravabet Ba Chin Az Oloviat haye Vizhe e Siasate Khareji e Dowlat e Ayande Ast" ["The Development of Relations with China Is One of the Special Political Priorities of the Next Government"], *Hamshahri Online*, June 26, 2013.

[93] "Larinjani Dar Daneshgah e Motale'at e Khareji e Pekan Sokhanrani MiKonad" ["Larinjani Speaks at the Beijing Foreign Studies University"], Iranian Students' News Agency, October 29, 2013.

fled Iran after the imposition of sanctions, but Chinese businesses have adopted what can be more accurately described as a holding pattern. China has decreased its purchase of Iranian oil and has refrained from additional investment in light of stringent sanctions, but the nuclear agreement will allow it to increase trade ties with Iran.

In some ways, China is better placed than other powers for exploiting the nuclear agreement. Beijing voted for United Nations Resolution 1929, paving the way for stronger international and unilateral sanctions against Iran. And China has largely complied with United Nations and U.S. sanctions. But China is more likely to be seen by Iran as having adopted a "softer" approach toward Iran when compared with the United States, France, United Kingdom, and even Russia. The Western members of the P5+1 have been assertive in increasing the pressure on Iran, and Russia, while initially opposed to greater sanctions, has largely played a supportive role. China, on the other hand, has been relatively passive in the P5+1 process and has followed the group's collective decisions. In addition, China remains Iran's number-one energy and commercial partner despite sanctions. Therefore, the Rouhani government is likely to view China as a major source of future economic growth for Iran. Since his election, Rouhani and his officials have made several gestures to strengthen relations with Beijing.

In May 2014, Rouhani attended the Conference on Interaction and Confidence Building Measures in Asia (CICA) summit in Shanghai,[94] where he again met bilaterally with his Chinese counterpart and Iranian businessmen living in China, calling for a further expansion of Iran's economic links with the country.[95]

---

[94] "Aghaz e Ejlase Saran e CICA Dar Shanghai e Chin Ba Hozur e Doktor Rouhani" ["Rouhani Present at Start of Leaders' Meetings at CICA in Shanghai, China"], President.ir, May 21, 2014; "Takid e Roosai Jomhure Iran Va Chin Bar Tose'e e Hame Janbe e Monasebat Mian e Do Keshvar" ["Leaders of Iranian and Chinese Republics Emphasize Development of Bilateral Relations"], President.ir, May 22, 2014.

[95] "President Prior to His Departure to China: Iran's Economic Ties with East/China Is Important to Iran," President.ir, May 20, 2014; "Hozur e Rouhani Dar Neshast e CICA/ Didar Ba Saran e Rusiye Va Chin Dar Shanghai" ["Rouhani Present at CICA Meeting/ Meeting with Russian and Chinese Leaders in Shanghai"], *Aftab News*, April 29, 2014.

Rouhani may in particular look to China's Silk Road initiative as an engine for economic growth. No doubt in response to the much-vaunted U.S. New Silk Road, the ambitious Silk Road Economic Belt aims to strengthen regional ties along its network and constitutes "not just an economic trade route, but a community with 'common interests, fate, and responsibilities.'"[96]

The Silk Road Economic Belt is itself one of the best indications of the importance that China places on ties with its Central and West Asian neighbors. Beijing signed an intensive series of bilateral agreements with these countries in the lead up to the CICA summit, covering energy, investment, and cultural exchanges.[97] Though some Chinese theorists and intellectuals have been sensitive to the implications of calling this a "go west" strategy,[98] it is clear that China takes these relationships seriously and has moved to strengthen and expand them.

In stark contrast to its U.S. alternative, the new Chinese Silk Road will also conspicuously include Iran.[99] One proposed route would enter Iran from Turkmenistan and move along the southern shore of the Caspian Sea, exiting at Iran's border with northern Iraq.[100] Another route that has been discussed would enter Iran from Pakistan and exit at Iran's border with southern Iraq.[101]

On a larger scale, the peaceful resolution of the Iranian nuclear crisis would allow China to integrate Iran more closely into its eco-

---

[96] Shannon Tiezzi, "China's 'New Silk Road' Vision Revealed," *The Diplomat*, May 9, 2014b. See also "Ahiai e Rah e Abrisham Hadaf e Bargozari e Namayeshgah Moshtarak e Iran Va Chin Ast" ["The Revival of the Silk Road Is the Goal of Holding a Joint Iranian and Chinese Exhibition"], Tasnim News Agency, August 12, 2014.

[97] Lauren Dickey, "China Takes Steps Toward Realizing Silk Road Ambitions," *China Brief*, Vol. 14, No. 11, June 4, 2014.

[98] Xuetong Yan, "Silk Road Economic Belt Shows China's New Strategic Direction: Promoting Integration with Its Neighbors," Carnegie-Tsinghua Center for Global Policy, February 27, 2014.

[99] Tiezzi, 2014b.

[100] Tiezzi, 2014b.

[101] David Daokui Li, Ming Feng, Jinjian Shi, Zhen He, and Wen Liu, "Silk Road Economic Belt: Prospects and Policy Recommendations," working paper, Beijing: Center for China in the World Economy, Tsinghua University, May 20, 2014.

nomic sphere. For example, Beijing is considering investment in a gas pipeline network connecting Iran to China through Turkmenistan and Kazakhstan. Bypassing the sea route would make China less vulnerable to U.S. naval interference over its energy resources.[102]

Another potential avenue for China-Iran economic and geopolitical cooperation is the Shanghai Cooperation Organization (SCO). Iran has been hoping to become a full member of the SCO for some time. The SCO (composed of China, Russia, Kazakhstan, Kyrgyzstan, Tajikistan, and Uzbekistan) is mostly dominated by China and Russia and has facilitated China's rise as the predominant power in Central Asia.

The Ahmadinejad government had boasted that Iran did not need the West and would instead pursue a vaguely defined foreign policy focusing on the East. The SCO became a focus of Ahmadinejad's outreach to the East.[103] As a security organization led by Russia and China, SCO was seen by Ahmadinejad as a means for Iran to counter the U.S. presence in the region and to escape its isolation.

However, Ahmadinejad failed in 2008 and 2010 to gain Iranian membership into the SCO. Although the SCO aims to balance against U.S. activities in Central Asia, member organizations were put off by Ahmadinejad's bellicose rhetoric toward the United States.[104] Furthermore, the relatively secular SCO member countries were wary of Iran's Islamist ideology. Iran has remained an observer state since 2005, without becoming a full member. This may be motivated by China and Russia's reluctance to expand membership to other major players; in addition to the two powers, the SCO is composed of relatively small states. Iran is not a great power on the scale of China or Russia, but it does have significant cultural and political influence in Central Asia and could become a competitor for China in the future. However,

---

[102] Samir Tata, "US, Iran and China: An Emerging Strategic Triangle," The International Relations and Security Network, January 30, 2014.

[103] Shahram Akbarzadeh, "Iran and the Shanghai Cooperation Organization: Ideology and Realpolitik in Iranian Foreign Policy," *Australian Journal of International Affairs*, Vol. 69, No. 1, 2015.

[104] Akbarzadeh, 2015.

Chinese analysts explained that Iran "would be next" to join the SCO after India and Pakistan's entry.[105]

Iran's participation in the SCO could strengthen Chinese interests in Central Asia and throughout the Muslim world. Beijing sees Iran as playing a potentially important role in muting Muslim criticism of China's suppression of separatist Uighurs.

The Chinese government faces growing instability in Xinjiang province, which is inhabited by Muslim Uighurs, a people of Turkic origin who claim widespread discrimination by the Han-dominated central government in Beijing. While China's suppression of the Uighurs has sparked condemnation from some quarters in Iran, especially among senior Shi'a clerics in Qom, the Islamic republic has thus far tactfully refrained from calling attention to this issue out of deference to Chinese sensitivities.[106]

Much as it did for the Russians in Chechnya, Iran is likely to protect China from international Islamic repercussions at the Organization of the Islamic Conference and instead offer only bland condemnations of "extremist" violence in Xinjiang.[107] In 2007, Supreme Leader Ayatollah Khamenei's website warned Iranians against criticizing China for suppression of Uighurs because doing so would undermine Iran-China ties.[108] The Rouhani government is likely to ignore the Uighur issue in order to focus on improving relations with China.

Beijing is also likely to look to Iran to buttress its interests in Afghanistan, as both nations have a shared interest in Afghanistan's stability. China, which maintains a 50-mile border with Afghanistan, has invested $3.5 billion in the Aynak copper mine and has been extracting oil from the Amu Darya basin since 2012. And Iran is concerned about the resurgence of the Taliban and other anti-Iranian groups. The

---

[105] Discussions with Chinese analysts, Beijing and Shanghai, September 8–15, 2014.

[106] Oppositional figures inside Iran, however, have spoken; see Robert F. Worth, "Clerics Fault a Mute Iran as Muslims Die in China," *New York Times*, July 13, 2009.

[107] "Iran Condemns Violence in Xinjiang, China," Islamic Republic News Agency, July 30, 2014.

[108] Akbarzadeh, 2015.

Iranian government is also worried about the massive flow of Afghan drugs into Iran.

China shares these concerns and also sees a social threat in Afghanistan's drug exports through Iran;[109] China has highlighted the issue at multiple SCO summits and has pledged its support in combating the problem.[110] China is aware of its own vulnerabilities in combating narcotics and sees regional cooperation as crucial given the intrinsically international nature of the problem.[111]

China and Iran have also announced the formation of a joint task force to battle drugs, money laundering, human trafficking, and passport fraud.[112] While the prosecution of money laundering cases will likely be sporadic given Iran's deep reliance on opaque and obfuscatory banking, its concern with narcotics is real. Long ignored and hidden, the astonishing scope and scale of drug addiction in Iran has become increasingly apparent in recent years,[113] and the government has made a growing point of combating the problem.[114]

The Rouhani government will likely view China not just as a geostrategic partner but as a potential military one as well. The Ahmadinejad years led to Iran's economic isolation and also the unwillingness of Russia and China to sell major weapon systems to Tehran. Russia canceled the sale of the sophisticated S-300 surface-to-air missile system

---

[109] Murray Scot Tanner, *China Confronts Afghan Drugs: Law Enforcement Views of "The Golden Crescent,"* Arlington, Va.: CNA China Studies, March 2011.

[110] "SCO Summit Is Held in Tashkent Hu Jintao Attends and Delivers an Important Speech to the Summit," Embassy of the People's Republic of China in the United States of America, June 11, 2010.

[111] Tanner, 2011.

[112] "Tashkil e Goruh haye Amaliati e Moshtarak e Iran va Chin Baray e Mobareze Ba Mavad e Mokhader" ["Formation of Joint Iranian-Chinese Working Groups to Combat Drugs"], *Tasnim News*, July 5, 2013.

[113] "The Other Religion: Why So Many Young Iranians Are Hooked On Hard Drugs," *The Economist*, August 17, 2013.

[114] "Afzayesh e Amar e Masraf e Mavad e Mokhader e Sanaty Mian e Javanan va Zanan/ Hal e Ma'zal Eshteghal Mohemtarin Rahkar e Mobareze ba E'tiad" ["Statistical Rise in Drug Use Among Youth and Women/Solving Employment Problems the Most Important Approach in Combating Addiction"], Mehr News, undated.

to Iran because of pressure from Washington and Tel Aviv. And China, once a major weapon supplier to Iran, has mostly ceased its defense and security ties with the Iranian government.

The nuclear agreement could change all of that by legitimizing the sale of weapons to the Rouhani government, although Iran will face a conventional arms embargo for five years following the agreement's implementation. And growing strains between China and the United States could convince Beijing to strengthen defense and security ties with Tehran. This does not mean that China will consider Iran an ally or even a close military partner anytime soon. Rather, China may increase defense ties with Iran, by selling it more-advanced systems, for example, if the nuclear accord makes Iran appear to be a more responsible international actor.[115]

Conclusion

China and Iran are natural partners on many levels. China does not have a history of intervention in Iran, as do Western countries, such as the United Kingdom and the United States. Moreover, Beijing does not critique the Iranian government's domestic politics. Both Iran and China are developing nations that fear U.S. power in their neighborhoods. And both have what the other needs; Iran has enormous energy resources, while China is a source of technology, investments, and perhaps even military hardware. However, there is a growing perception in Iran of overdependence on China. Rouhani and his centrist and reformist supporters are eager to improve Iran's ties with Europe and to some extent even seek détente with the United States. Iran's rehabilitation under Rouhani could allow it to become less dependent on China economically and militarily. And it would open Iran to what its people and many of its elite view as superior goods and technology.

China's economic opportunities in Iran could increase with the easing or lifting of sanctions, but this is not guaranteed. Western companies reentering Iran would compete with the Chinese. Western

[115] Harold and Nader, 2012.

consumer goods are perceived by Iranians to be of better quality, and Western energy companies have superior technology. Increased Iranian oil output would bring global oil prices down, which is ultimately to the benefit of China. However, in the short term, China would lose the lucrative oil-pricing agreements that Iran was forced to enter into because of the sanctions, as well as the barter agreement for inferior Chinese products.

China values close relations with Iran but will want to make sure that the two countries are not perceived by the West as being too close. Beijing had limited its economic interactions with Iran because of Tehran's nuclear ambitions and the resulting sanctions. While China benefits from Iran's reliance on it, and shares the Islamic republic's desire to balance against the United States in the Persian Gulf, Beijing will only go so far in challenging Washington. After all, China's trade volume with the United States dwarfs Iran-China trade, and China has strong relations with Iranian foes, such as Israel and Saudi Arabia.[116] Furthermore, China wants to be seen as a responsible international stakeholder and, therefore, will be susceptible to Western pressure to limit ties with Iran in the event of a failed nuclear agreement.[117] While Iran and China may be close, they nevertheless face hurdles in assuming a stronger and more strategic partnership.

---

[116] Harold and Nader, 2012.

[117] Liao, 2013.

CHAPTER FIVE

Whither the Wary Dragon? Implications for the United States

How does Beijing view the Middle East? The region is only growing in importance to China. Indeed, the Middle East is fast becoming China's most important region outside of the Asia-Pacific. The reasons relate to great Chinese insecurity over energy, domestic instability, and a perception that the Middle East is a key geostrategic region of the world. For Beijing, the Middle East is an extension of its western borderlands in Central Asia—China's extended periphery.

Beijing under Xi Jinping—much like the Obama administration in Washington—is seeking a more geostrategically balanced foreign and security policy. While the United States is rebalancing in the Asia-Pacific, China is working toward a westward rebalance to correct what has tended to be a lopsided eastward overemphasis in terms of economic development and national security protection.

This Beijing rebalance, however, is neither a reaction to the Obama administration's own rebalance nor a new phenomenon; China is in the midst of a geostrategic rebalance that can be seen as a continuation of efforts to focus greater attention toward the Middle East since the mid-1990s. China views the Middle East as increasingly important, and Beijing has growing worries over chronic instability in the region (especially in Syria and Iraq). This rebalance includes trends that are evident and important for U.S. policymakers to understand. China is driven to protect its greater interests in the region by leveraging its relationships with key regional powers—in particular

- Saudi Arabia: viewed as a stable state keen to partner with China and capable of committing to long-term economic cooperation
- Iran: viewed as a close but complicated Chinese partner, which, although under sanctions and international pressure, may serve as a greater economic and geostrategic partner after the nuclear agreement.

Mismatch in the Middle East

China is a wary dragon, very cautious, alarmed about becoming embroiled in Middle East controversies or getting too close to any one country in the region. And China has refused to put forward an explicit Middle East policy or strategy with specifics for fear of raising the ire of one or more states in the region. Under Xi, Beijing does not possess an articulated Middle East strategy. Instead, China publicly subsumes its approach toward the region under the rubric of a broader "march west" concept, in an effort to rebalance its center of gravity and skewed national security posture. Essentially, this effort is an extension of Beijing's approach toward Central Asia, which emphasizes expanding economic ties—especially commerce and enhanced transportation links. Using direct allusions to centuries-old overland trade routes—collectively known as the Silk Road—Chinese leaders have promoted a vision of shared economic development and mutual benefit across land and by sea. As a result of these concerns, Chinese analysts and leaders view the Middle East as China's extended periphery. A clear indication of this schema is the repeated use of the term *greater Middle East*. The term refers to not just the Middle East but South and Central Asia as well.[1] This "march west" strategy is focused on China's strength—economics—and channeled through the One Belt, One Road initia-

---

[1] Liu Zhongmin, "Shi shui Zhong Dong: Bianjuxiade Zhongguo waijiao" ["Testing the Waters in the Middle East: China's Foreign Relations Under Turbulent Change"], *Shijie Zhishi* [*World Affairs*], No. 5, 2013, p. 48. As one Chinese analyst notes, the term *greater*

tive. Beijing seeks to build on its successes in Central Asia and replicate this positive track record in the Middle East and elsewhere.

Beijing's growing interests and increasing engagement in the region highlight both the impressive achievements and the limitations of China's Middle East strategy. Specifically, there is a mismatch between China's interests, corresponding objectives, and the types of instruments and mechanisms Beijing is willing and able to devote toward attaining these objectives. China's main interests in the Middle East and related objectives presume a peaceful and stable environment. However, Beijing is heavily focused on economic efforts, with limited diplomatic involvement and token military contributions. An environment of peace and stability in the Middle East is far from the reality on the ground. Maintaining a modicum of stability requires the vigorous efforts of outside powers to reassure allies and deter and, if necessary, fight adversaries. This is a role that China to date has not been willing or able to play. The United States is the primary actor fulfilling this role and, for the foreseeable future, China seems amenable to this state of affairs and more than willing to free ride. China and the United States have overlapping interests in the Middle East—both desire stability and unfettered access to energy.[2] However, China does not make the prevention of "the development, proliferation, or use of weapons of mass destruction" a top priority the way that the United States does.[3] This is not to say that China opposes these objectives; rather, these are much lower priorities for China. Furthermore, Beijing does not support Washington's goals of advancing democracy and human rights in the Middle East.

Beijing views Washington's foreign policy with suspicion, sensing that the United States targets dictatorships and is intent on overthrowing the CCP. At a minimum, China perceives the United States as

---

Middle East was originally coined by the George W. Bush administration. The Chinese have embraced the term but have given it a distinctive Chinese slant. Li, 2004.

[2] According to the 2015 *National Security Strategy*, the United States desires "stability and peace in the Middle East" and "the free flow of energy from the region to the world." Barack Obama, *National Security Strategy*, Washington, D.C.: White House, February 2015, p. 26.

[3] Obama, 2015, p. 26.

trying to contain or at least constrain Beijing's burgeoning economic and military power. However, while Beijing sees itself as locked in a great power rivalry with Washington, it nevertheless desires to maintain an overall climate of cordial and cooperative U.S.-Chinese relations, as well as promote stability in the Middle East. Washington, meanwhile, is suspicious of Beijing's intentions but is receptive to greater Chinese contributions to regional security. However, China is neither likely to provide significant support to the United States nor likely to contest or directly challenge the U.S. role in the Middle East.

This mismatch among interests, commitment, and goals is likely to continue. China's strategy toward the Middle East is best characterized as that of a wary dragon—eager to engage commercially with the region and remain on good terms with all states in the Middle East but most reluctant to deepen its engagement, including strengthening its diplomatic and security activities, beyond the minimum required to make money and ensure energy flows. Beijing also works to prevent public criticism of China's policies, especially toward Chinese Muslims, and receive recognition of its great-power status. The result is a China that is growing in importance in the Middle East but a country that has become an economic heavyweight, while it persists as a diplomatic lightweight, and is likely to remain a military featherweight in the region for the foreseeable future.

China is reluctant to become too militarily embroiled in the Middle East. It is much easier to stay aloof, remain on good terms with all states of the region, and let the United States do all the heavy lifting. And most Chinese analysts do not anticipate that the United States will completely withdraw from the region.[4] But Beijing does feel pressure from Washington and faces expectations from countries in the Middle East to do more. When National Security Advisor Susan Rice visited Beijing in early September 2014, she reportedly urged China to contribute more to Middle East security and join the fight against ISIL. In the immediate aftermath of her visit, Chinese analysts appeared uncer-

---

[4] See, for example, Niu Xinchun, "'Nengyuan duili' wei shixian ding Zhong Dong libukai" ["'Energy Independence' Not to Be Achieved (the U.S.) Inseparably Bound to the Middle East"], *Shijie Zhishi* [*World Affairs*], No. 1, 2014b.

tain about how to respond and about what specific support the Obama administration was seeking from China.[5]

The Elephant in the Room

For China, the elephant in the room is the United States. The precondition for continued economic growth, as well as trade and investment, is a peaceful environment in the region. This presupposes a stable Middle East. China is not in a position to provide or even contribute in any substantial way beyond token efforts, such as providing United Nations peacekeeping troops and a small naval task force for anti-piracy patrols. Beijing recognizes that someone else must provide for regional peace and stability and finds the United States an acceptable actor.

What does China's expanding presence in the Middle East mean for enduring U.S. interests in the region? Does China's growing influence pose a threat to U.S. security partnerships with the GCC and the U.S. military posture in the Middle East? To date, Chinese influence in the region has largely been economic. But growing trade and investment also gives Beijing increased geopolitical stature, and China's significant energy needs makes the Middle East of paramount importance to China's economy—it would be hard pressed to watch idly if insecurity threatened its access to these resources. At the same time, countries in the region perceive U.S. economic and political clout in the Middle East as either stagnant or declining, and concerns in the region about Washington's staying power as an ally or security partner have risen. The interest by such countries as Saudi Arabia in expanding defense cooperation with China is driven less by strong enthusiasm for a greater Chinese military involvement in the region than it is by growing uncertainties about Washington's security commitment. The reality is very different—the United States remains firmly committed to the Middle East: This is evident from the Obama administration's actions, statements, and key documents, including the *National Secu-*

---

[5] On U.S. pressure: author interviews, September 2014; on regional expectations: Li Weijian, 2014, pp. 33–34.

rity Strategy issued in 2015 and the *Quadrennial Defense Review* issued in 2014. And the next administration is unlikely to deviate much from this level of commitment.

While one U.S. analyst noted that some observers assume that, eventually, "China will supplant the United States as the kingdom's principal security guarantor,"[6] such an outcome seems most improbable at least in the short to medium term. There are two reasons for this judgment: First, Washington does not indicate any intention to withdraw from the Persian Gulf; second, Beijing does not demonstrate signs of an eagerness to replace the United States as the region's main security player. China cannot provide the same range of high-technology weaponry, and its armed forces do not possess the level of interoperability or the extensive combat and noncombat operational experience of U.S. forces. Nevertheless, in the unlikely event that Washington downgrades its commitment to the Middle East or Persian Gulf region, Chinese-Saudi ties might become closer.

Expanded security cooperation between China and Saudi Arabia is not necessarily a cause for U.S. alarm. Indeed, such cooperation may be helpful and contribute toward a more stable regional environment. However, secretive arms sales and backdoor deals are likely to create anxiety and distrust among other countries in the region and hence could undermine U.S. interests in the Persian Gulf and wider Middle East. Enhanced security cooperation between China and Iran would likely be alarming, but not if the relationship was transparent and in the aftermath of the nuclear agreement.

But Beijing does not have a sterling record as an enduring or reliable ally, nor does the PLA have a history of effective partnerships with other militaries to meet long-term goals. While there are certainly some exceptions—notably, North Korea and Pakistan—even these exceptions have been plagued with tensions and turmoil. In other words, China does not have anything like the array of durable military allies and partner militaries of the United States. The U.S. military is accustomed to exercising and working alongside allied and friendly militaries, while the PLA is not. Furthermore, should China develop mili-

[6] Lippman, 2013, p. 256. The analysis in this paragraph is derived from pp. 256–258.

tary allies and partners, it is not clear how quickly they could become effective at operating together. Exercising with other militaries is still a relatively new concept—the first military exercise the PLA conducted with another country's armed forces was in 2003 with Kyrgyzstan. Although China now routinely conducts bilateral and multilateral exercises, these are mostly small scale and uncomplicated.[7] It is difficult to imagine China mounting a major and complex multilateral undertaking to counter ISIL forces in Iraq and Syria or even approaching such an effort as Operations Desert Shield and Desert Storm, in which the United States was able to assemble a coalition of different countries.

What types of indicators would signal a qualitative upgrading of Chinese security relationships in the Middle East? Indicators might include the following:

- initiation of bilateral exercises or multilateral exercises with specific countries or security groupings
- expanded arms sales of conventional or strategic weaponry with specific states
- expanded military exchanges and defense diplomacy with particular states
- formal basing agreements—currently, China does not have any formal basing agreements in the Middle East.

Recommendations

At a grand strategic level, Washington should adopt a two-pronged strategy where Beijing and the Middle East are concerned. First, the United States should encourage China, along with other Asian powers, to become more involved in efforts to improve regional stability.[8] Second, Washington should work to reassure partners of its enduring

---

[7] For an overview of China's involvement in SCO exercises, see Scobell, Ratner, and Beckley, 2014, pp. 37–40.

[8] The 2015 *National Security Strategy* states: "We [the United States] seek cooperation on shared regional and global challenges" (Obama, 2015, p. 24).

security commitment to the region. In conjunction with these political moves, the Pentagon should apply strategic and operational concepts toward China for this highly volatile region of enormous geostrategic importance to the United States, and in so doing create options to work with China and build more-positive, cooperative global relationships between China and other states. This means being open to new thinking and new approaches of working to protect key U.S. interests in the Middle East, including "improving [the U.S.] ability to cooperate in concrete, practical areas" with China's PLA.[9]

Encourage China

The United States should welcome some expanded Chinese security engagement in the Middle East. However, despite the considerable importance of the region to China's economy and its growing power, China is hesitant to engage. Nevertheless, the United States seeks reliable and "capable partners" to address the long-term challenges of managing security in the Middle East (and elsewhere).[10] Enhanced roles for China and other Asian powers could have positive benefits for the United States and its allies. Moreover, the Middle East is in turmoil, and a "struggle for power is underway [*sic*] among and within many states" in the region.[11] Not just China but other Asian states—India, Japan, and South Korea—have growing energy and economic interests in the Middle East, and each can make security contributions to promote regional stability, especially if they can cooperate with each other.[12] While some of these Asian states harbor mutual suspicions and distrust, and have unresolved territorial disputes in their own neighborhoods, there are possibilities for real cooperation to promote common interests in such locations as the Middle East.

---

[9] U.S. Department of Defense, *Quadrennial Defense Review*, Washington, D.C., 2014, p. 17.

[10] Obama, 2015, p. 3.

[11] Obama, 2015, p. 5.

[12] On the growing economic involvement of these Asian states in the Middle East, see Kemp, 2010; and Davidson, 2010.

Expanded security cooperation between China, Saudi Arabia, and other GCC countries is not necessarily a cause for U.S. alarm. Such cooperation may be helpful and contribute toward a more stable regional environment. Chinese security cooperation with Iran is more problematic, but there are no signs that Beijing is eager for an alliance with Tehran, despite the September 2014 Chinese-Iranian naval exercises in the Persian Gulf.[13] Indeed, continued but transparent security ties between Beijing and Tehran as the nuclear deal is implemented could serve to reassure Iran that it is on the right path and that a partner of long-standing has not abandoned it.

The region is undergoing tumultuous changes, and the contours of the future security environment are far from clear. Beijing has become perhaps the most important capital outside the region, other than Washington. Under the circumstances, the United States should be receptive to cooperating with China in the Middle East and Persian Gulf where interests coincide, while being prepared to counter China if necessary when interests conflict. China is unlikely to attempt to dominate the region, even in the event of rising U.S.-Chinese tensions over the Middle East because the wary-dragon strategy persists. Rather, instability in the Middle East can provide a venue for greater Chinese-U.S. engagement, and cooperation between China and its Asian neighbors might ultimately help alleviate rising tensions in East Asia.

Reassure Partners

While encouraging China to take a more active role in the region, the United States should continue to take a leading security role in the Persian Gulf. A military confrontation between the United States and China in the Middle East is highly implausible. Indeed, China does not even have sufficient forces in the region to mount such an effort, not to mention the political will or desire to directly challenge the United States in the Middle East or Persian Gulf. The major threats to the region come from the hybrid forces of ISIL, along with other

---

[13] Ankit Panda, "China and Iran's Naval Exercise," *The Diplomat*, September 23, 2014.

terrorist groups, and the assertiveness of Iran.[14] The strategic focus of the United States in the region continues to be strengthening partner capabilities and deterring and containing Iran. In this effort, the U.S. Army has key roles in developing relationships with partner Arab ground forces and in maintaining a forward presence in Kuwait. This role is not limited to Army forces either; reassuring partners in the face of real proximate threats is a core joint mission for all component commands in U.S. Central Command.

Washington should follow up on the recent initiatives launched by then–Secretary of Defense Chuck Hagel. In May 2014, Hagel was in Jeddah, Saudi Arabia, to attend a ministerial-level session of the U.S.-GCC Defense Dialogue. Hagel's visit followed trips to Saudi Arabia by then–Deputy Secretary of State William Burns in February and a visit by Obama in March. Each of these senior U.S. officials reportedly stressed the strength of the continued U.S. security commitment to the Persian Gulf, which is manifested in a variety of ways, such as approximately 35,000 troops in some dozen bases around the region and the sale of high-tech weaponry, including missile defense systems, to the six GCC member states.[15] The Army's contribution to these ongoing efforts is significant and should continue.

At the operational level, the Obama administration is working to persuade Bahrain, Kuwait, Oman, Qatar, the United Arab Emirates, and Saudi Arabia to develop a regional missile defense shield. The United States, according to Hagel, desires to enhance GCC "interoperability and . . . sophisticated multilateral force development."[16] The U.S. Army has a role to play in facilitating the introduction of the

---

[14] The analysis in this paragraph draws on the *Quadrennial Defense Review* (U.S. Department of Defense, 2014, p. 33), the *National Security Strategy* (Obama, 2015, p. 26), and work by RAND's Michael Johnson conducted for the U.S. Army.

[15] Paul Richter, "U.S. Aims to Bolster Ties with Persian Gulf States," *Los Angeles Times*, February 20, 2014.

[16] Rachel Oswald, "Hagel Urges Gulf States to Collaborate on Missile Defense," Global Security Newswire, May 15, 2014.

PAC-3 missiles to Saudi Arabia under the terms of a $1.75 billion deal, authorized in October 2014.[17]

China's greater involvement in the Middle East may come in light of tensions between the United States and its regional allies. However, the United States is set to remain the security guarantor of choice for Saudi Arabia and the smaller Gulf States. China's growing economic, political, and even security ties with these countries will not necessarily harm U.S. interests. If anything, greater cooperation between the United States, China, and other Asian powers on Middle East security could lead to a lessening of tensions in other areas, such as East Asia.

At the moment, there does not appear to be a demand for additional U.S. forces to counter increased Chinese commitments to the region. China is not eager to make such commitments, although the United States seems to want some increased level of Chinese contributions to help increase stability in the region. Should instability affecting Middle East energy output materialize, China would have difficult decisions to make regarding whether to increase its security involvement. This would likely be contingent on U.S. actions, with China deferring to U.S. intervention as it has in the past, should the United States choose to intervene. Cooperative efforts prior to such an event could lead to better outcomes that do not raise tensions between the United States and China.

---

[17] Jeremy Binnie, "US Approves Saudi PAC-3 Sale," *Jane's Defence Weekly*, October 2, 2014.

Abbreviations

CCP	Chinese Communist Party
CICA	Conference on Interaction and Confidence Building Measures in Asia
CNPC	China National Petroleum Corporation
GCC	Gulf Cooperation Council
GDP	gross domestic product
IRBM	intermediate-range ballistic missile
ISIL	Islamic State in Iraq and the Levant
NATO	North Atlantic Treaty Organization
P5+1	five permanent members of the United Nations Security Council, plus Germany
PLA	People's Liberation Army
PRC	People's Republic of China
ROC	Republic of China
SABIC	Saudi Basic Industries Corporation
SCO	Shanghai Cooperation Organization
SIPRI	Stockholm International Peace Research Institute

TIV	trend indicator value
WTO	World Trade Organization

References

"About SABIC in China," SABIC, January 20, 2012. As of October 14, 2015: http://sabic.51job.com/asia_china.php

"Afzayesh e Amar e Masraf e Mavad e Mokhader e Sanaty Mian e Javanan va Zanan/Hal e Ma'zal Eshteghal Mohemtarin Rahkar e Mobareze ba E'tiad" ["Statistical Rise in Drug Use Among Youth and Women/Solving Employment Problems the Most Important Approach in Combating Addiction"], Mehr News, undated. As of September 22, 2014: http://www.mehrnews.com/detail/News/2353228

"Aghaz e Ejlase Saran e CICA Dar Shanghai e Chin Ba Hozur e Doktor Rouhani" ["Rouhani Present at Start of Leaders' Meetings at CICA in Shanghai, China"], President.ir, May 21, 2014. As of October 31, 2014: http://www.president.ir/fa/77660

"Ahiai e Rah e Abrisham Hadaf e Bargozari e Namayeshgah Moshtarak e Iran Va Chin Ast" ["The Revival of the Silk Road Is the Goal of Holding a Joint Iranian and Chinese Exhibition"], Tasnim News Agency, August 12, 2014.

Akbarzadeh, Shahram, "Iran and the Shanghai Cooperation Organization: Ideology and Realpolitik in Iranian Foreign Policy," *Australian Journal of International Affairs*, Vol. 69, No. 1, 2015, pp. 88–103.

Albright, David, and Andrea Stricker, "Iran's Nuclear Program," in United States Institute of Peace, *The Iran Primer*, Washington, D.C., updated September 2015. As of October 14, 2015: http://iranprimer.usip.org/resource/irans-nuclear-program

Alterman, Jon B., "China's Soft Power in the Middle East," in Carolina G. McGiffert, ed., *Chinese Soft Power and Its Implications for the United States: Competition and Cooperation in the Developing World*, Washington, D.C.: Center for Strategic and International Studies, 2009.

———, "The Vital Triangle," in Bryce Wakefield and Susan L. Levenstein, eds., *China and the Persian Gulf: Implications for the United States*, Washington, D.C.: Woodrow Wilson International Center for Scholars, 2011, pp. 27-37

Alterman, Jon B., and John W. Garver, *The Vital Triangle: China, the United States, and the Middle East*, Washington, D.C.: Center for Strategic and International Studies, 2008.

"Bi Keyfiat Budan e Kola haye Chini Tabligh e Gharb Ast" ["The Poor Quality of Chinese Goods is Western Propaganda"], Digarban.com, March 11, 2012. As of October 31, 2014:
http://www.digarban.com/node/5413

Binnie, Jeremy, "US Approves Saudi PAC-3 Sale," *Jane's Defence Weekly*, October 2, 2014.

Calabrese, John, "From Flyswatters to Silkworms: The Evolution of China's Role in West Asia," *Asian Survey*, Vol. 30, No. 9, September 1990, pp. 862–876.

———, "Saudi Arabia and China Extend Ties Beyond Oil," *China Brief*, Vol. 5, No. 20, October 2005.

"Chang Wanquan Meets with Crown Price of Saudi Arabia," *China Military Online*, March 17, 2014.

Chen, Xiangming, and Ivan Su, "A Different Global Power? Understanding China's Role in the Developing World," *The European Financial Review*, June 2014.

"China and Saudi Arabia," website of the PRC Embassy in Jeddah, August 26, 2004.

"China Exports PLZ45 155mm Guns to Saudi Arabia," *Kanwa Asian Defense Review*, August 2008.

"China Floods Iran with Cheap Consumer Goods in Exchange for Oil," *Guardian*, February 20, 2013. As of October 31, 2014:
http://www.theguardian.com/world/iran-blog/2013/feb/20/china-floods-iran-cheap-consumer-goods

"China Issues 6-Point Statement on Syria," CCTV.com, March 4, 2012. As of October 7, 2014:
http://english.cntv.cn/program/newsupdate/20120304/107425.shtml

"China Opens Missile Plant in Iran," *UPI*, April 23, 2010. As of October 31, 2014:
http://www.upi.com/Business_News/Security-Industry/2010/04/23/China-opens-missile-plant-in-Iran/UPI-82791272037022

"China 'Resolutely Opposes' U.S. Sanctions on Missile Parts Supplier," Reuters, April 30, 2014. As of October 31, 2014:
http://www.reuters.com/article/2014/04/30/us-china-usa-iran-idUSBREA3T07720140430

"China to Finance 7 Iranian Methanol Projects," Fars News Agency, June 14, 2014. As of October 31, 2014:
http://english.farsnews.com/newstext.aspx?nn=13930324000818

"Chinese Militants Get Islamic State 'Terrorist Training': Media," Reuters, September 22, 2014. As of October 31, 2014:
http://www.reuters.com/article/2014/09/22/us-china-xinjiang-idUSKCN0HH10J20140922

"Chinese President Arrives in Riyadh at Start of 'Trip of Friendship, Cooperation,'" *Xinhua*, February 10, 2009.

Chu Shulong, "Bei Fei Zhong Dong jushi yu Zhongguo" ["China and the Changing Situation in the Middle East and North Africa"], *Xiandai Guoji Guanxi* [*Contemporary International Relations*], No. 3, 2011.

Chu Shulong and Jin Wei, *Zhongguo waijiao zhanlue he zhengce* [*China's Foreign Affairs Strategy and Policy*], Beijing: Shishi Chubanshe, 2008.

Chulov, Martin, "Barack Obama Arrives in Saudi Arabia for Brief Visit with Upset Arab Ally," *Guardian*, March 28, 2014. As of October 31, 2014:
http://www.theguardian.com/world/2014/mar/28/barack-obama-saudi-arabia-arab-ally

Cooper, Helene, "Saudi Arabia Says King Won't Attend Meetings in U.S.," *New York Times*, May 10, 2015.

Crane, Brent, "A Tale of Two Chinese Muslim Minorities," *The Diplomat*, August 22, 2014. As of September 26, 2014:
http://thediplomat.com/2014/08/a-tale-of-two-chinese-muslim-minorities/

Davidson, Christopher, *The Persian Gulf and Pacific Asia: From Indifference to Interdependence*, New York: Columbia University Press, 2010.

Demick, Barbara, "Xinjiang Attacks Attributed to China's Uighurs Grow in Sophistication," *Los Angeles Times*, May 22, 2014. As of May 24, 2014:
http://www.latimes.com/world/asia/la-fg-car-bombs-china-uighur-20140522-story.html

Dickey, Lauren, "China Takes Steps Toward Realizing Silk Road Ambitions," *China Brief*, Vol. 14, No. 11, June 4, 2014.

Dickey, Lauren, and Helia Ighani, "Iran Looks East, China Pivots West," *The Diplomat*, August 25, 2014.

Dorraj, Manochehr, and James English, "China's Strategy for Energy Acquisition in the Middle East: Potential for Conflict and Cooperation with the United States," *Asian Politics & Policy*, Vol. 4, No. 2, April 2012, pp. 173–191.

———, "The Dragon Nests: China's Energy Engagement of the Middle East," *China Report*, Vol. 49, No. 1, February 2013, pp. 43–67.

Downs, Erica, "China-Gulf Energy Relations," in Bryce Wakefield and Susan L. Levenstein, eds., *China and the Persian Gulf: Implications for the United States*, Washington, D.C.: Woodrow Wilson International Center for Scholars, 2011, pp. 62–78.

———, "Cooperating with China on Iran," The German Marshall Fund of the United States, January 2012.

Duchatel, Mathieu, Oliver Brauner, and Zhou Hang, *Protecting China's Overseas Interests: The Slow Shift Away from Non-Interference*, SIPRI Policy Paper No. 41, Stockholm: Stockholm International Peace Research Institute, June 2014.

"Enteghad az Dowlat beh Dalile 'Vagozaariye Bazaare Iran beh Chiin'" ["Criticism of Administration for 'Handing Iranian Market Over to China'"], *Deutsche Welle*, June 6, 2012.

Erdbrink, Thomas, and Chris Buckley, "China and Iran to Conduct Joint Naval Exercises in the Persian Gulf," *New York Times*, September 21, 2014. As of October 31, 2014:
http://www.nytimes.com/2014/09/22/world/middleeast/china-and-iran-to-conduct-joint-naval-exercises-in-the-persian-gulf.html

Erickson, Andrew S., and Austin M. Strange, *No Substitute for Experience: Chinese Antipiracy Operations in the Gulf of Aden*, China Maritime Study No. 10, Newport, R.I.: U.S. Naval War College, November 2013.

"Fehreste 170 Kalaaye Varedaatiye Bi-Keyfiyat" ["List of 170 Poor Quality Imported Goods"], *Tabnak*, August 24, 2010. As of October 31, 2014:
http://www.tabnak.ir/fa/news/116070

Gao Zugui, "Dabianju shenhua beijingxia Zhongguo yu Zhong Dong guanxi de fazhan" ["Development of China's Relations with the Middle East in the Context of Profound Changes"], *Heping yu Fazhan* [*Peace and Development*], No. 1, 2014, pp. 39-47.

Garver, John, "China-Iran Relations: Cautious Friendship with America's Nemesis," *China Report*, Vol. 49, No. 1, February 2013, pp. 69–88.

Garver, John W., and Fei-ling Wang, "China's Anti-Encirclement Struggle," *Asian Security*, Vol. 6, No. 3, September–December 2010, pp. 238–261.

Gill, Bates, and Chin-hao Huang, "China's Expanding Presence in UN Peacekeeping Operations and Implications for the United States," in Roy Kamphausen, David Lai, and Andrew Scobell, eds., *Beyond the Strait: PLA Missions Other Than Taiwan*, Carlisle Barracks, Pa.: U.S. Army War College Strategic Studies Institute, 2009, pp. 99–126.

Harold, Scott Warren, and Alireza Nader, *China and Iran: Economic, Political, and Military Relations*, Santa Monica, Calif.: RAND Corporation, OP-351-CMEPP, 2012. As of September 4, 2014:
http://www.rand.org/pubs/occasional_papers/OP351.html

Holz, Heidi, and Kenneth Allen, "Military Exchanges with Chinese Characteristics: The People's Liberation Army Experience with Military Relations," in Roy Kamphausen, David Lai, and Andrew Scobell, eds., *The PLA at Home and Abroad: Assessing the Operational Capabilities of China's Military*, Carlisle Barracks, Pa.: U.S. Army War College Strategic Studies Institute, 2010, pp. 430–480.

House, Karen Elliott, *On Saudi Arabia: Its People, Past, Religion, Fault Lines—and Future*, New York: Knopf, 2012.

"Hozur e Rouhani Dar Neshast e CICA/Didar Ba Saran e Rusiye Va Chin Dar Shanghai" ["Rouhani Present at CICA Meeting/Meeting with Russian and Chinese Leaders in Shanghai"], *Aftab News*, April 29, 2014. As of September 4, 2014:
http://aftabnews.ir/fa/news/241771

Information Office of the State Council, *The Diversified Employment of China's Armed Forces*, Beijing, April 2013.

International Atomic Energy Agency, *Implementation of the NPT Safeguards Agreement in the Islamic Republic of Iran*, Vienna, November 10, 2003.

International Crisis Group, *China's Growing Role in UN Peacekeeping*, Asia Report No. 166, Brussels, April 17, 2009. As of October 31, 2014:
http://www.crisisgroup.org/~/media/Files/asia/north-east-asia/166_chinas_growing_role_in_un_peacekeeping.pdf

"Iran, China to Sign $2b Deal on Dams," *Press TV*, May 10, 2007. As of October 31, 2014:
http://edition.presstv.ir/detail/9403.html

"Iran > Procurement," in *Jane's Sentinel Security Assessment—The Gulf States*, IHS Jane's, September 10, 2014. As of September 10, 2014:
https://janes.ihs.com/CustomPages/Janes/DisplayPage.aspx?DocType=Reference&ItemId=+++1303499&Pubabbrev=GULF

"Iran Condemns Violence in Xinjiang, China," Islamic Republic News Agency, July 30, 2014. As of October 31, 2014:
http://www.irna.ir/en/News/2732753/Politic/Iran_condemns_violence_in_Xinjiang,_China

"Iran Views China Ties as Strategic: Official," *PressTV*, April 8, 2014. As of October 31, 2014:
http://www.presstv.com/detail/2014/04/08/357664/iran-hails-strategic-ties-with-china/

Jacobs, Andrew, "Tiananmen Square Anniversary Prompts Campaign of Silence," *New York Times*, May 28, 2014. As of October 31, 2014:
http://www.nytimes.com/2014/05/28/world/asia/tiananmen-square-anniversary-prompts-campaign-of-silence.html

Kahl, Colin H., Melissa G. Dalton, and Matthew Irvine, *Atomic Kingdom: If Iran Builds the Bomb, Will Saudi Arabia Be Next?* Washington, D.C.: Center for a New American Security, February 2013.

Kemp, Geoffrey, *The East Moves West: India, China, and Asia's Growing Presence in the Middle East*, Washington, D.C.: Brookings Institution, 2010.

Lakshmanan, Indira A.R., and Pratish Narayanan, "India and China Skirt Iran Sanctions with 'Junk for Oil,'" Bloomberg, March 30, 2012. As of September 4, 2014:
http://www.bloomberg.com/news/2012-03-29/india-and-china-skirt-iran-sanctions-with-junk-for-oil-.html

"Larinjani Dar Daneshgah e Motale'at e Khareji e Pekan Sokhanrani MiKonad" ["Larinjani Speaks at the Beijing Foreign Studies University"], Iranian Students' News Agency, October 29, 2013.

Levine, Steven I., "China in Asia: The PRC as a Regional Power," in Harry Harding, ed., *China's Foreign Relations in the 1980s*, New Haven, Conn.: Yale University Press, 1984, pp. 107–145.

Lewis, Jeffrey, "Saudi Arabia's Strategic Dyad," *Arms Control Wonk*, July 15, 2013. As of October 31, 2014:
http://lewis.armscontrolwonk.com/archive/6688/saudi-arabias-strategic-dyad

———, "Why Did Saudi Arabia Buy Chinese Missiles?" *Foreign Policy*, January 30, 2014.

Lewis, John W., Hua Di, and Xue Litai, "Beijing's Defense Establishment: Solving the Arms-Export Enigma," *International Security*, Vol. 15, No. 4, Spring 1991, pp. 87–109.

Li, David Daokui, Ming Feng, Jinjian Shi, Zhen He, and Wen Liu, "Silk Road Economic Belt: Prospects and Policy Recommendations," working paper, Beijing: Center for China in the World Economy, Tsinghua University, May 20, 2014. As of October 31, 2014:
http://intl.ce.cn/specials/zxxx/201405/26/P020140526515434111874.pdf

Li Weijian, "Zhong Dong zai Zhongguo zhanlue zhong de zhongyaoxing ji shuangbian guanxi" ["Bilateral Relations Between China and the Middle East and the Importance of the Middle East in China's Strategy"], *XiYa Feizhou* [*West Asia and Africa*], No. 6, 2004.

———, "Dangqian Zhong Dong anquan jushi ji dui Zhongguo Zhong Dong waijiao yingxiang" ["Current Security Situation in the Middle East and Implications for China's Middle East Diplomacy"], *Guoji guancha* [*International Observer*], No. 3, 2014.

Liao, Janet Xuanli, "China's Energy Diplomacy and Its 'Peaceful Rise' Ambition: The Cases of Sudan and Iran," *Asian Journal of Peacebuilding*, Vol. 1, No. 2, 2013, pp. 197–225.

Lippman, Thomas W., *Saudi Arabia on the Edge: The Uncertain Future*, Washington, D.C.: Potomac Books, 2013.

Liu Zhongmin, "Shi shui Zhong Dong: Bianjuxiade Zhongguo waijiao" ["Testing the Waters in the Middle East: China's Foreign Relations Under Turbulent Change"], *Shijie Zhishi* [*World Affairs*], No. 5, 2013.

Ma, Wayne, "China Imports Record Amount of Iranian Crude," *Wall Street Journal*, July 21 2014. As of October 31, 2014:
http://online.wsj.com/articles/china-imports-record-amount-of-iranian-crude-1405946504

MacLean, William, "Iran Seeks Banned Nuclear Items, Uses China Trader for Missile Parts: U.S.," Reuters, March 17, 2014. As of September 4, 2014:
http://www.reuters.com/article/2014/03/17/us-iran-nuclear-supplies-idUSBREA2G1EF20140317

Medeiros, Evan S., *Reluctant Restraint: The Evolution of China's Nonproliferation Policies and Practices, 1980–2004*, Stanford, Calif.: Stanford University Press, 2007.

———, *China's International Behavior: Activism, Opportunism, and Diversification*, Santa Monica, Calif.: RAND Corporation, MG-850-AF, 2009. As of October 14, 2015:
http://www.rand.org/pubs/monographs/MG850.html

Meick, Ethan, *China's Reported Ballistic Missile Sale to Saudi Arabia: Background and Potential Implications*, Washington, D.C.: U.S.-China Economic and Security Review Commission, June 16, 2014.

Mouawad, Jad, "China's Growth Shifts the Geopolitics of Oil," *New York Times*, March 19, 2010. As of October 31, 2014:
http://www.nytimes.com/2010/03/20/business/energy-environment/20saudi.html

Nathan, Andrew J., and Andrew Scobell, *China's Search for Security*, New York: Columbia University Press, 2012.

Naughton, Barry J., "The Western Development Program," in Barry J. Naughton and Dali Yang, eds., *Holding China Together: Diversity and National Integration in the Post-Deng Era*, New York: Cambridge University Press, 2004, pp. 253–295.

Niu Xinchun, "China's Interests in and Influence over the Middle East," trans. Haibing Xing, *Contemporary International Relations*, Vol. 24, No. 1, January/February 2014a, pp. 37–58.

———, "'Nengyuan duili' wei shixian ding Zhong Dong libukai" ["'Energy Independence' Not to Be Achieved (the U.S.) Inseparably Bound to the Middle East"], *Shijie Zhishi* [*World Affairs*], No. 1, 2014b.

Obama, Barack, *National Security Strategy*, Washington, D.C.: White House, February 2015.

Oswald, Rachel, "Hagel Urges Gulf States to Collaborate on Missile Defense," Global Security Newswire, May 15, 2014.

"The Other Religion: Why So Many Young Iranians Are Hooked on Hard Drugs," *The Economist*, August 17, 2013. As of September 4, 2014: http://www.economist.com/news/middle-east-and-africa/21583717-why-so-many-young-iranians-are-hooked-hard-drugs-other-religion

Panda, Ankit, "China and Iran's Historic Naval Exercise," *The Diplomat*, September 23, 2014. As of November 6, 2015: http://thediplomat.com/2014/09/china-and-irans-historic-naval-exercise/

"President Prior to His Departure to China: Iran's Economic Ties with East/China Is Important to Iran," President.ir, May 20, 2014. As of September 4, 2014: http://president.ir/en/77630

Qian Xuewen, "Zhong Dong jubian dui Zhongguo haiwai liyi de yingxiang" ["Impact of Middle East Turmoil on China's Overseas Interests"], *Alabo Shijie Yanjiu* [*Arab World Studies*] No. 6, November 2012, pp. 50–51.

Richter, Paul, "U.S. Aims to Bolster Ties with Persian Gulf States," *Los Angeles Times*, February 20, 2014. As of October 31, 2014: http://articles.latimes.com/2014/feb/20/world/la-fg-wn-us-gulf-states-20140220

Richter, Paul, and Alex Rodriguez, "Chinese Bank Pulls Out of Pakistan-Iran Pipeline Project," *Los Angeles Times*, March 14, 2012. As of October 31, 2014: http://articles.latimes.com/2012/mar/14/world/la-fg-pakistan-china-pipeline-20120315

Said, Summer, "Saudi Arabia, China Sign Nuclear Cooperation Pact," *Wall Street Journal*, January 16, 2012. As of October 31, 2014: http://online.wsj.com/articles/SB10001424052970204468004577164742025285500

"Saudi Arabia Admits to Purchase of Chinese DF-21 Missile," *Want China Times*, September 22, 2014. As of October 31, 2014: http://www.wantchinatimes.com/news-subclass-cnt.aspx?id=20140922000059&cid=1101

"Saudi Arabia and the United States: Awkward Relations," *The Economist*, March 29, 2014.

"Saudi Arabia Signs Deal for China's Pterodactyl Drone," *Want China Times*, May 7, 2014. As of October 31, 2014: http://www.wantchinatimes.com/news-subclass-cntaspx?id=20140506000088&cid=1101

Saul, Jonathan, "Chinese Firms Drop Iran as Latest U.S. Sanctions Bite," Reuters, July 1, 2013.

Schenker, David, "China's Middle East Footprint," *Los Angeles Times*, April 27, 2013.

Scobell, Andrew, "China Ponders Post-2014 Afghanistan: Neither 'All in' nor Bystander," *Asian Survey*, Vol. 55, No. 2, March–April 2015, pp. 325–345.

Scobell, Andrew, and Scott W. Harold, "An 'Assertive' China? Insights from Interviews," *Asian Security*, Vol. 9, No. 2, 2013, pp. 111–131.

Scobell, Andrew, Ely Ratner, and Michael Beckley, *China's Strategy Toward South and Central Asia: An Empty Fortress*, Santa Monica, Calif.: RAND Corporation, RR-525-AF, 2014. As of October 14, 2015:
http://www.rand.org/pubs/research_reports/RR525.html

"SCO Summit Is Held in Tashkent Hu Jintao Attends and Delivers an Important Speech to the Summit," Embassy of the People's Republic of China in the United States of America, June 11, 2010. As of September 4, 2014:
http://www.china-embassy.org/eng//zgyw/t708530.htm

Seznec, Jean-Francois, "China and the Gulf in 2010: A Political Economic Survey," in Bryce Wakefield and Susan L. Levenstein, eds., *China and the Persian Gulf: Implications for the United States*, Washington, D.C.: Woodrow Wilson International Center for Scholars, 2011, pp. 54–61.

Shambaugh, David, *China Goes Global: The Partial Power*, Oxford, UK: Oxford University Press, 2013.

Sheives, Kevin, "China Turns West: Beijing's Contemporary Strategy Towards Central Asia," *Pacific Affairs*, Vol. 79, No. 2, Summer 2006, pp. 205–224.

Shichor, Yitzhak, *The Middle East in China's Foreign Policy, 1949–1977*, New York: Cambridge University Press, 1979.

———, "Fundamentally Unacceptable yet Occasionally Unavoidable: China's Options on External Interference in the Middle East," *China Report*, Vol. 49, No. 1, 2013, pp. 25–41.

Shirk, Susan, *China: Fragile Superpower*, Oxford, UK: Oxford University Press, 2007.

Simpfendorfer, Ben, *The New Silk Road: How a Rising Arab World Is Turning Away from the West and Rediscovering China*, Basingstoke, UK: Palgrave Macmillan, 2009.

"SIPRI Arms Transfers Database—Methodology," web page, Stockholm International Peace Research Institute, undated. As of November 20, 2015:
http://www.sipri.org/databases/armstransfers/background/background_default

Solmirano, Carina, and Pieter D. Wezeman, "Military Spending and Arms Procurement in the Gulf States," SIPRI Fact Sheet, Stockholm: Stockholm International Peace Research Institute, October 2010.

Subler, Jason, "China's ZTE Says It Basically Dropped Iran Business," Reuters, April 18, 2013. As of September 4, 2014:
http://www.reuters.com/article/2013/04/18/us-zte-iran-idUSBRE93H0A820130418

Al-Sudairi, Mohammend Turki, *China in the Eyes of the Saudi Media*, GRC Gulf Papers, Jeddah, Saudi Arabia: Gulf Research Center, February 2013.

Sun, Yun, "Iran and Asia 1: China Is the Quiet Giant," in *The Iran Primer*, Washington, D.C.: United States Institute of Peace, January 29, 2014. As of October 31, 2014:
http://iranprimer.usip.org/blog/2014/jan/29/iran-and-asia-1-china-quiet-giant

"Takid e Roosai Jomhure Iran Va Chin Bar Tose'e e Hame Janbe e Monasebat Mian e Do Keshvar" ["Leaders of Iranian and Chinese Republics Emphasize Development of Bilateral Relations"], President.ir, May 22, 2014. As of September 4, 2014:
http://www.president.ir/fa/77824

"Takid e Vaziraee e Defa' e Iran va Chin bar Gostaresh e Hamkari haye Defa'ee Tehran va Pekan" ["Tehran and Beijing—Iranian and Chinese Defense Secretaries Emphasize Increase in Defense Cooperation"], Fars News Agency, May 5, 2014. As of October 31, 2014:
http://www.farsnews.com/newstext.php?nn=13930215000326

Tanner, Murray Scot, *China Confronts Afghan Drugs: Law Enforcement Views of "The Golden Crescent,"* Arlington, Va.: CNA China Studies, March 2011.

"Tashkil e Goruh haye Amaliati e Moshtarak e Iran va Chin Baray e Mobareze Ba Mavad e Mokhader" ["Formation of Joint Iranian-Chinese Working Groups to Combat Drugs"], *Tasnim News*, July 5, 2013. As of September 4, 2014:
http://www.tasnimnews.com/Home/Single/91768

Tata, Samir, "Recalibrating American Grand Strategy: Softening U.S. Policies Toward Iran in Order to Contain China," *Parameters*, Vol. 42, No. 4, 2013, pp. 47–58.

———, "US, Iran and China: An Emerging Strategic Triangle," The International Relations and Security Network, January 30, 2014. As of October 31, 2014:
http://www.isn.ethz.ch/Digital-Library/Articles/Detail/?lng=en&id=176024

Tiezzi, Shannon, "Saudi Arabia, China's Good Friend," *The Diplomat*, March 14, 2014a. As of October 31, 2014:
http://thediplomat.com/2014/03/saudi-arabia-chinas-good-friend/

———, "China's 'New Silk Road' Vision Revealed," *The Diplomat*, May 9, 2014b. As of September 4, 2014:
http://thediplomat.com/2014/05/chinas-new-silk-road-vision-revealed/

———, "Chinese Nationals Evacuate Yemen on PLA Navy Frigate," *The Diplomat*, March 30, 2015. As of November 6, 2015:
http://thediplomat.com/2015/03/chinese-nationals-evacuate-yemen-on-pla-navy-frigate/

"Tose'e Ravabet Ba Chin Az Oloviat haye Vizhe e Siasate Khareji e Dowlat e Ayande Ast" ["The Development of Relations with China Is One of the Special Political Priorities of the Next Government"], *Hamshahri Online*, June 26, 2013. As of September 4, 2014:
http://www.hamshahrionline.ir/details/220457

"U.S. Accuses Chinese Man Of Breaching Iran Nuclear Sanctions," BBC, April 4, 2014. As of October 31, 2014:
http://www.bbc.com/news/world-us-canada-26892568

U.S. Department of Defense, *Quadrennial Defense Review*, Washington, D.C., 2014.

U.S. Department of Justice, "'Karl Lee' Charged in Manhattan Federal Court with Using a Web of Front Companies to Evade U.S. Sanctions," Office of Public Affairs, April 29, 2014. As of September 4, 2014:
http://www.justice.gov/opa/pr/2014/April/14-nsd-450.html

U.S. Energy Information Administration, "Country Analysis Brief: China," Washington, D.C., February 4, 2014.

———, "Country Analysis Brief: Iran," Washington, D.C., July 21, 2014.

"US Targets Weapons, Oil Sanctions Evaders," in *The Iran Primer*, Washington, D.C.: United States Institute of Peace, April 29, 2014. As of September 2014:
http://iranprimer.usip.org/blog/2014/apr/29/us-targets-weapons-oil-sanctions-evaders

Van Ness, Peter, "China as a Third World State: Foreign Policy and Official National Identity," in Lowell Dittmer and Samuel S. Kim, eds., *China's Quest for National Identity*, Ithaca, N.Y.: Cornell University Press, 1993, pp. 194–214.

"Vision and Actions Are Jointly Building Silk Road Economic Belt and 21st Century Maritime Silk Road," news release, National Development and Reform Commission, Ministry of Foreign Affairs, Ministry of Commerce of the People's Republic of China with State Council authorization, March 28, 2015.

Wang Jisi, "'Xijin': Zhongguo diyuan zhanlue de zai pingheng" ["'Marching West': China's Geostrategic Rebalance"], *Huanqiu Shibao* [*Global Times*], October 17, 2012. As of October 31, 2014:
http://opinion.huanqiu.com/opinion_world/2012-10/3193760.html

Wehrey, Frederic, "After King Abdullah, Continuity," Carnegie Endowment for International Peace, January 23, 2015. As of January 28, 2015:
http://carnegieendowment.org/syriaincrisis/?fa=58810

Wong, Jasper, "Saudi-China Relations Emblematic of China's New Foreign Policy Challenges," *The Interpreter*, July 18, 2014. As of October 31, 2014:
http://www.lowyinterpreter.org/post/2014/07/18/
Saudi-China-relations-Chinas-new-foreign-policy-challenges.aspx

Worth, Robert F., "Clerics Fault a Mute Iran as Muslims Die in China," *New York Times*, July 13, 2009. As of September 23, 2014:
http://www.nytimes.com/2009/07/14/world/middleeast/14iran.html

Worth, Robert F., and C. J. Chivers, "Seized Chinese Weapons Raise Concerns on Iran," *New York Times*, March 2, 2013. As of September 4, 2014:
http://www.nytimes.com/2013/03/03/world/middleeast/
seized-arms-off-yemen-raise-alarm-over-iran.html?_r=0

Wu Bingbing, "Strategy and Politics in the Gulf as Seen from China," in Bryce Wakefield and Susan L. Levenstein, eds., *China and the Persian Gulf: Implications for the United States*, Washington, D.C.: Woodrow Wilson International Center for Scholars, 2011, pp. 10–26.

Wu Jiao and Zhang Yunbi, "Xi Proposes a 'New Silk Road' with Central Asia," *China Daily*, September 8, 2013. As of October 31, 2014:
http://usa.chinadaily.com.cn/china/2013-09/08/content_16952304.htm

"Xi Jinping Holds Talks with President Hassan Rouhani of Iran, Stressing to Promote China-Iran Friendly Cooperation to New High," Ministry of Foreign Affairs of the People's Republic of China, May 22, 2014.

Yan, Xuetong, "Silk Road Economic Belt Shows China's New Strategic Direction: Promoting Integration with Its Neighbors," Carnegie-Tsinghua Center for Global Policy, February 27, 2014. As of September 4, 2014:
http://carnegietsinghua.org/2014/02/27/silk-road-economic-belt-shows-china-s-new-strategic-direction-promoting-integration-with-its-neighbors

Zhao Hong, "China's Dilemma on Iran: Between Energy Security and a Responsible Rising Power," *Journal of Contemporary China*, Vol. 23, No. 87, 2014, pp. 408–424.

Zhao Jingfang, "Pojie nengyuan anquan kunjing: waijiao he junshi shouduan" ["Solving Energy Difficulties: Diplomatic and Military Methods"], *Shijie Zhishi* [*World Affairs*], No. 18, 2012, pp. 44–53.

"Zhongguo 'xijin' yong pingheng zhanlue zhilu" ["China's 'March West' Guiding Balancing Strategy"], *Qiushi* [*Seeking Truth*], April 22, 2014. As of October 31, 2014:
http://www.qstheory.cn/gj/gjsspl/201404/t20140422_342588.htm